MARVEL NEMESIS™
RISE OF THE IMPERFECTS

Prima Official Game Guide

Brad Anthony

Prima Games
A Division of Random House, Inc.
3000 Lava Ridge Court, Suite 100
Roseville, CA 95661
1-800-733-3000
www.primagames.com

The Prima Games logo is a registered trademark of Random House, Inc., registered in the United States and other countries. Primagames.com is a registered trademark of Random House, Inc., registered in the United States. Prima Games is a division of Random House, Inc.

© 2005 Electronic Arts Inc. Electronic Arts, EA, Imperfects, Rise of the Imperfects and related characters are trademarks or registered trademarks of Electronic Arts Inc. in the U.S. and/or other countries. Imperfects and related characters © 2005 Electronic Arts Inc. All rights reserved.
MARVEL, and all related characters and trademarks and the distinctive likenesses thereof are trademarks of Marvel Characters, Inc. and are used with permission. © 2005 Marvel Characters, Inc. All right reserved. www.marvel.com. Licensed by Marvel Characters, Inc. All other trademarks are the property of their respective owners. EA™ is an Electronic Arts™ brand.

No part of this book may be reproduced or transmitted in any form or by any means, electronic or mechanical, including photocopying, recording, or by any information storage or retrieval system without written permission from Electronic Arts Inc.

Product Manager: Jill Hinckley
Editor: Kate Abbott
Copy Editor: Asha Johnson
Design & Layout: Marc W. Riegel

Please be advised that the ESRB Ratings icons, "EC," "E," "E10+," "T," "M," "AO," and "RP" are trademarks owned by the Entertainment Software Association, and may only be used with their permission and authority. For information regarding whether a product has been rated by the ESRB, please visit www.esrb.org. For permission to use the Ratings icons, please contact the ESA at esrblicenseinfo.com.

Important: Prima Games has made every effort to determine that the information contained in this book is accurate. However, the publisher makes no warranty, either expressed or implied, as to the accuracy, effectiveness, or completeness of the material in this book; nor does the publisher assume liability for damages, either incidental or consequential, that may result from using the information in this book. The publisher cannot provide information regarding game play, hints and strategies, or problems with hardware or software. Questions should be directed to the support numbers provided by the game and device manufacturers in their documentation. Some game tricks require precise timing and may require repeated attempts before the desired result is achieved.

ISBN: 0-7615-5147-6
Library of Congress Catalog Card Number: 2005904207
Printed in the United States of America

05 06 07 08 GG 10 9 8 7 6 5 4 3 2 1

Table of Contents

Acknowledgements

Special thanks to Willie Loh, Dan Ayoub, Mike Lee, and the rest of the EA team for tirelessly answering my many questions and providing invaluable support! To the Prima Games team, you all rock! As always, very special thanks to my mom, Barb, who, when I was a kid, worked hard to give me $40/week so I could hang out in the arcades and do what I loved to do—and I'm still doing it!

D1200122

introduction

history

As any leading scientist would do, Van Roekel tried to stay impartial when the newcomers arrived on his home planet. His society welcomed them *en masse* and he continued his work as one of the leading intellects of his people. His research into DNA, sociology, biology, and art established him as something of a Leonardo da Vinci of his race. As the new inhabitants settled into life on his home planet, the seeds of oppression were sewn. Life as they knew it changed more rapidly as one would expect, everything from infrastructure to politics, and Van Roekel's people knew that things would never be the same—at least not by any peaceful resolutions. He knew they must escape to develop a strategy, a weapon that would allow them to retake their planet by force. Van Roekel and a massive contingent of scientific and military staff fled their world to find their ultimate answer at any cost.

It took decades and monumental steps, but finally Van Roekel had the research faculties required and test subjects were "convinced" to be part of the development program—each for their own specific reasons. In his secret lab underneath New York, Van Roekel killed many of his genetic test subjects before implementing a new plan that recruited the likes of Solara, Johnny Ohm, Hazmat, Brigade, Fault Zone, and The Wink. His new prototypes were successful in their own rights but yet imperfect. From this research came Paragon—the ultimate fusion of human aggression and alien technology; the perfect warrior. A weapon like her, when mass produced, would surely reclaim Van Roekel's home planet and return it to rightful rule.

His race was by nature quite nonaggressive, and Van Roekel knew he could not shine as a warrior leader using his natural demeanor and genetic predisposition. In order to rectify this issue, he created the Minuteman armor. This suit bypassed his natural passivism and made him powerful and ruthless. Now, not only could he lead his army of perfect warriors into battle on his home world, he could keep an iron fist ready to smash any challenges from his prototype group—The Imperfects.

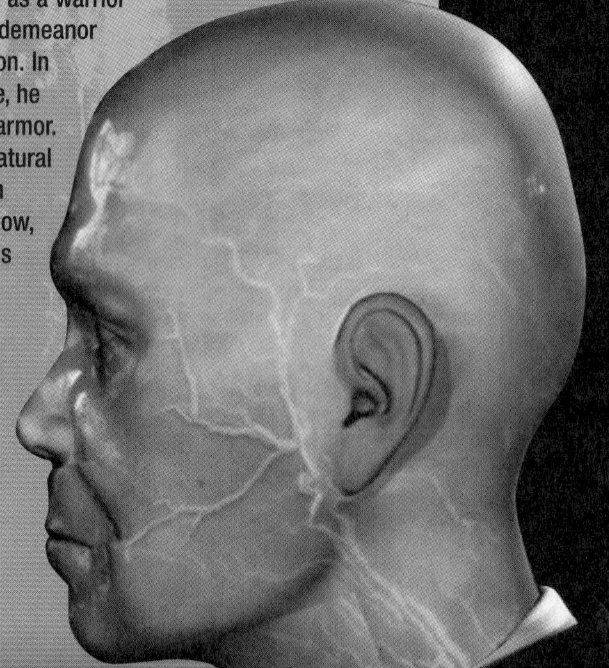

Van Roekel's Science

Turlin Neural Override

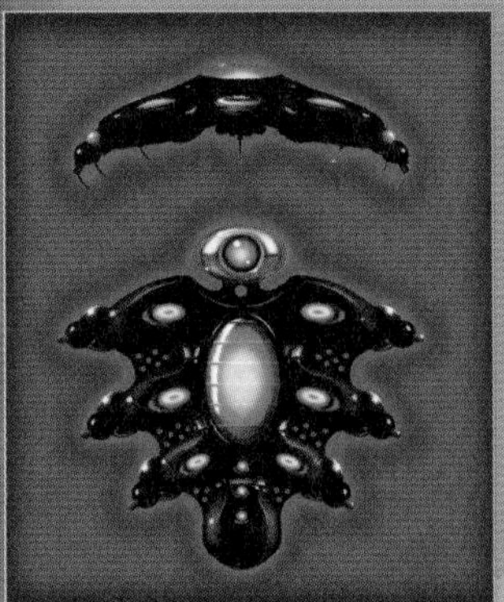

This sentient device is Van Roekel's nasty tool. It thrives on human adrenaline. Attaching itself to the nape of someone's neck, it sinks branching needles into the spinal column. By stimulating the limbic system, it causes the carrier to become extremely violent, thereby increasing the production of adrenaline. Given simple commands by Van Roekel, it uses the victim to carry out his nefarious deeds while, of course, always knowing where the host is and what he or she sees and hears.

Turlin Engine

The Turlin Engine is a completely amphibious flying machine that provides power and surveillance.

Van Roekel's Inventions

All Van Roekel's biotech research is done using these cloning and operating pods.

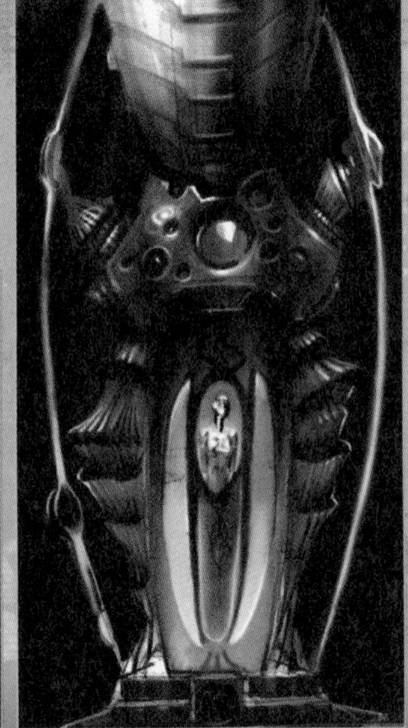

Background

Through the centuries, a displaced band of aliens, led by Dr. Niles Van Roekel, has been working to create an army of warriors to liberate his own world from oppression. Van Roekel scoured the universe to find a civilization that had the brutality and savagery necessary to help him reclaim his planet. And after centuries of patience he found that only one planet possessed the right species…Earth.

Van Roekel sought out Earth's mightiest creatures and decided to experiment on Marvel's superhero population. After several failed attempts, Van Roekel got fed up dealing with these pesky heroes. So he constructed a top-secret lab under the Museum of Modern Art in New York. In his effort to create the ultimate warrior he had six human test subjects merged with alien technology.

These were only imperfect "prototypes" that eventually would lead to the definitive creation—Paragon, a revolutionary killing machine. When completed, Paragon was to be mass-produced and sent back to rescue Van Roekel's home planet. Paragon, however, had other ideas. During a routine neural reprogramming session she escaped the facility and disappeard into the depths of New York City.

The aliens launched an offensive to get her back. Troops, vehicles, and warriors were sent to find her at any cost. Unfortunately, innocent human civilians were collateral damage in their quest. Marvel's bothersome heroes intervened to save the New Yorkers but inadvertently posed a threat to Van Roekel. He condemned them to death and dispatched his imperfect warriors to destroy them. Superheroes were sacrificed and cities collapsed in attempts to retrieve Paragon and move ahead with Van Roekel's liberation plan.

Now, Paragon must decide whether to honor her alien ancestry and save this desperate alien race—or lead a new team of pissed-off superheroes, "The Imperfects," to help Earth recover from this devastating battle.

Gameplay

General Movement and Combat

The universal control system used in *Marvel Nemesis* equalizes moves and abilities across the board for all characters—eliminating the need to memorize many different moves. This allows players to focus on the game, using the environment and its features as part of the fighting strategy. Here we cover all of the movement and combat maneuvers; look for the combos and move list at the end of the chapter.

Mobilty Move
Attack
Block
Superpower Modifier
Jump
Move, Horizontal Movement (flying)
Pick Up Object/ Throw Opponent

Walk

This is the basic form of ground movement. It is the slowest movement type and depends primarily on your character's movement or speed rating. Walking uses none of your superpower meter.

Mobility Move

Each character has a specific mobility move. For ground-based individuals, like Daredevil, it's a run. Other characters can wall-run, swing, or fly. This movement type slowly eats up your superpower meter.

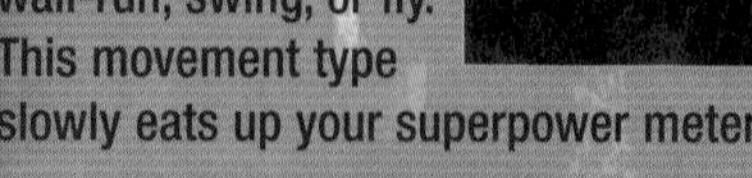

Super Mobility Move

Some characters have a super mobility move that allows a bit more flexibility in certain environments. Wolverine and a few other characters use this technique to wall-hang. Super mobility moves also eat up your superpower meter.

Jump

The basic jump can get you out of a sticky situation, or it can put you in harm's way if you're careless. Leaping around has its advantages, however. Use the elevation difference to add variety to your tactics and attacks.

Characters do two different types of jump attacks depending on whether they're going up (ascending) or down (descending) in the jump trajectory. While traveling upward in the jump, a hero may execute a backward flip kick. While on the way down, a hero alternately throws a downward axe kick.

Super Jump

All characters can super jump by using the superpower modifier while jumping. This uses up some of the superpower meter but the higher jump trajectory is quite valuable for getting across an area quickly—either toward or away from your opponent. For example, Thing's super jump is higher and farther than that of most characters, but it also eats up more of his superpower meter.

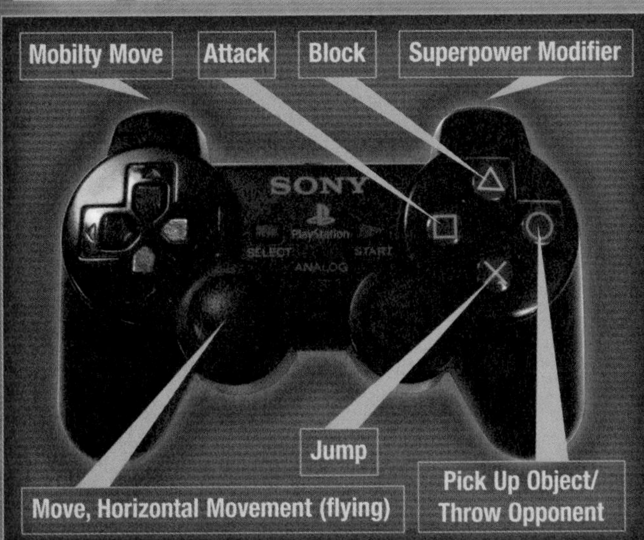

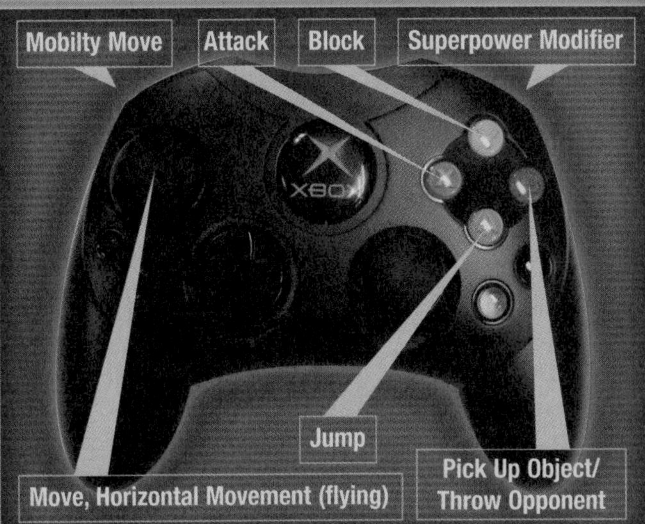

Note

Most moves aimed at opponents (attacks, throws, weapons, etc.) are assisted. This means you only need to hold the directional pad or thumb stick in the general direction of your opponent for the attacks to be aimed properly.

Block

Blocking is an essential skill, but a difficult one to master. Time your blocks well ahead of anticipated attacks—which is easier with projectiles and harder with close-up physical attacks. You can block in the middle of an opponent's regular strength or super attack combos.

Redirect

Redirect is an amazing ability, but it's the hardest to execute. You must press the block button at the exact moment of impact. You can redirect a physical attack, which can put your opponent off balance and allow you time to recover and launch a counterattack.

Dodge & Dodge Attacks

You can dodge forward, backward, left, and right by blocking and using the directional pad or thumb stick at the same time. Some characters flip, some roll, but they all use it to get out of the way.

Dodging is not just for evasion, though. All characters have special attacks they can execute from a dodge. Using a dodge and an attack close together makes your hero perform a dodging attack. Greatly improve this technique by using the superpower modifier.

Tip

Successful blocks add to your superpower meter.

Super Block

A super block is any normal block that is performed with the superpower modifier. During a super block you are completely invincible—but there is a drawback. A super block uses up your superpower meter at blistering speeds, so you can block like this for only a few seconds at most.

Tip

The best use of super block is when you expect your opponent to weapon at you (their ranged attacks). Note that super blocks do *not* rebound thrown objects back at your attacker.

Rising Attacks

Even the biggest heroes get knocked flat on their backs sometimes, but it doesn't mean you have to lie on the floor like a lump. This is where rising attacks come in very handy. Attack a nearby foe by pressing the attack button while lying prone.

Super Rising

The same applies to super rising attacks. From a prone position, press the attack and the superpower modifier buttons at the same time. This version of the rising attack commonly knocks back your opponent. Some characters like Venom have rising attacks that are considerably dangerous.

Carry

With all of the debris and weapons lying around, you'll want to pick some of it up. Use the carry/throw button to pick up any items your character is strong enough to lift. Everyone can pick up Class 1 objects, but only the most powerful heroes can pick up Class 3 objects, which also do the most damage of any weapon in the game.

Tip

Catch objects being thrown at you by hitting the carry/throw button just before impact. Successful catches add to your superpower meter.

Toss

Once you've got an object in hand, it's time to throw it at your unfortunate opponent. The controls are assisted, so you only have to be aiming in your foe's general direction when you press the carry/throw button again to launch your projectile attack. If you're standing really close to your opponent, instead of throwing the object, you just bean him over the head with it, which can be just as satisfying.

Tip

Alternately, if you've got an object in hand you can beat a downed opponent with it by using the attack button instead of tossing the object with the throw button.

Weapons and Props

Various items found around arenas can be used to wreak havoc on your opponents. These come in all shapes and sizes, from small pipes to huge radio towers. The important thing to note is which class they fall into and whether or not your chosen character can use them. The classes are outlined below:

WEAPON AND PROP CLASSES

CLASS	EXAMPLES	DAMAGE
Class 1	Barrels, alien props, lockers, air conditioners, phone booths	Low
Class 2	Garbage bins, computer terminals, forklifts, cars, taxis, concrete blocks	Medium
Class 3	Large fuel containers, radio towers, trucks, pillars, tanks	High

POLES

CLASS	EXAMPLES	DAMAGE
Class 1	Pipes, parking meters	Low
Class 2	Radio towers	High

Attack

All attacks and combinations are executed using the attack button. Some characters have better combos than others, but it depends entirely on their fictional attributes. Better fighters have better techniques and are able to pull off more impressive combos. In hand-to-hand fighting there is a noticeable difference between characters such as Wolverine and the Human Torch. Fighting style and depth is covered in the characters sections of "Marvel Heroes" and "The Imperfects."

Super Attack

When superpowers are added to physical attacks, they become much stronger and more dramatic—with the personal flair of our favorite characters. Execute your attack while also pressing the superpower modifier button to launch super attacks against your foes. Pay attention to your superpower meter, as using these abilities eats away at your superpower reserve (some much more than others).

Note

Attack combinations are interchangeable between regular and superpowered attacks. Practice throwing both types of attacks into a combination for interesting and more effective results. There are no character-specific combos so focus on learning the different attacks from various positions.

Tip

Air attack combos are very flashy ways to kick butt. One attack while ascending easily links into the second air attack while descending, for a two-hit combo.

Recovery

Every character in the game has a recovery move. When you're attacked and thrown through the air, destined for impact with obstacles or walls, press and hold the mobility and superpower buttons to allow your character to recover. These recovery moves save you from taking fall damage; however, they also eat up your SP meter—if your meter is too low, you can't recover at all.

Here's a breakdown of who has what recovery moves:

- **Fliers catch themselves in mid-air: Storm, Iron Man, Human Torch, Johnny Ohm, Solara, Roekel, Magneto**
- **Swingers go into a swing: Spider-Man, Daredevil, Venom, Hazmat**
- **Spider-Man and Venom will stick to the wall if they hit it while recovering.**
- **Sprinters/Wall Runners will catch themselves on the ground, or if they hit the wall, they perform a type of friction move and catch/attach themselves to the wall momentarily. This includes Wolverine, Thing, Brigade, Fault Zone, and Elektra.**
- **Teleporters (Paragon and The Wink) will teleport in mid-air.**

Rage

Rage mode is where the fun really begins. While enraged, a character has full superpower for 10 seconds for characters such as Iron Man and Human Torch, and up to 20 seconds for characters known for their rage such as Wolverine. This feature is based on character fiction.

Each attack you throw at an opponent is worth a certain number of points toward filling up the rage meter. That amount is character dependent, but it factors in the type of character. For example: The Thing's throwing attacks contribute more to his rage meter, while for Spider-Man it's his swinging attacks, and for Human Torch it's flying attacks, etc.

Note that you have approximately 10 seconds to activate Rage mode once the meter is full. Take advantage of it or the bonus is lost until you fill the meter again.

Throw

Throws are often the favorite part of a fight. The satisfaction you get from throwing an opponent through a wall or pillar keeps you grinning for days. Once you're close enough to grab your foe, hit the carry/throw button to execute a throw.

Super Throw

The super version of the throw causes more damage and tends to put a lot of distance between you and your opponent. This gives you time to regroup before the next attack. Or, follow up immediately to finish him off. Keep in mind that some characters like Spider-Man, Venom, Daredevil, Magneto, and others have long-range super throws and can grab hold of you from a distance.

Air Tackles

You can execute throws and super throws while in the air—these are otherwise known as air tackles. Your opponent must also be in the air, either jumping or flying, in order for this flashy and devastating move to work. Perform the throw the same way you would on the ground, but for much more dramatic effects and damage.

Health and Stamina

There are essentially two health meters, superimposed on top of one another. The stamina meter is lighter in color, and placed on top of the darker health meter. Stamina represents temporary losses and is affected by regular attacks. Stamina losses are regained based on the character's durability attribute. Health losses are permanent and are caused by superpower attacks, weapons, and throws.

When either of the meters (stamina or health) is reduced to near zero and the character is in Danger mode, you can perform a finishing move. This is one way to beat an opponent dramatically. The alternative is to continue to beat him or her down to zero health.

Finishing Moves

Every character has a finishing move and they are all performed the same way to maximize how easily they're used and enjoyed. When an opponent's health or stamina meter is low, they go into Danger mode. This is the time to strike! You must have at least one-quarter of your superpower meter full to perform a finishing move. If you have less than that, you'll just do an ordinary super throw.

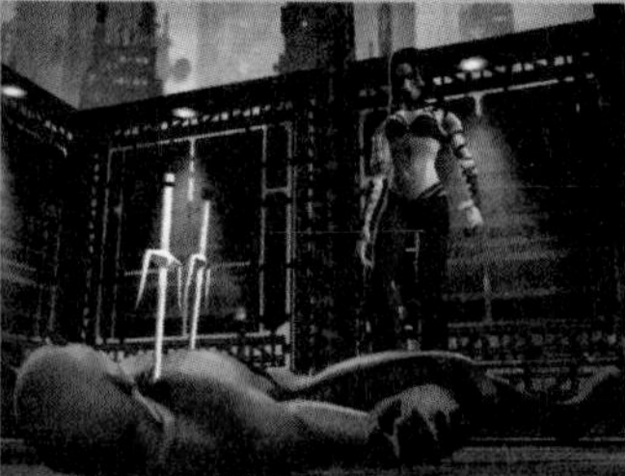

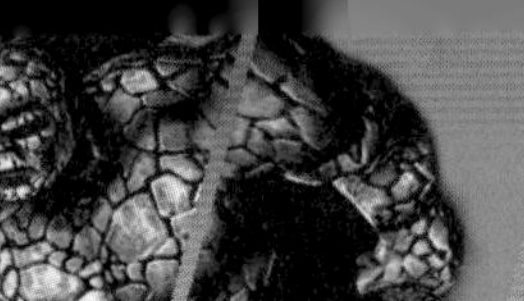

MOVE LIST

Move Type	*Xbox*	*PS2*	*NGC*
Attack	X	■	A
Super Attack	X+R	■+R1	A+R
Far Attack (from just out of melee distance)	X	■	A
Super Far Attack (from just out of melee distance)	X+R	■+R1	A+R
Throw	B	●	X
Super Throw	B+R	●+R1	X+R
Jumping Attack (ascending)	A, X	×, ■	B, A
Jumping Attack (descending)	A, X	×, ■	B, A
Super Jumping Attack (ascending)	A, X+R	×, ■+R1	B, A+R
Super Jumping Attack (descending)	A, X+R	×, ■+R1	B, A+R
Wall Run	D-pad+L	D-pad+L1	D-pad+L
Wall Run Attack (during wall run)	X	■	A
Wall Run Super Attack (during wall run)	X+R	■+R1	A+R
Wall Hang *	D-pad+L+R	D-pad+L1+R1	D-pad+L+R
Wall Hang Attack (during wall climb or hang) *	X	■	A
Wall Hang Super Attack	X+R	■+R1	A+R
Attack Stomp (against prone opponent)	X	■	A
Super Attack Stomp (against prone opponent)	X+R	■+R1	A+R
Rising Attack (from prone position)	X	■	A
Super Rising Attack (from prone position)	X+R	■+R1	A+R
Mobility Move (fly, swing, run)	L	L1	L
Mobility Attack (during mobility move)	X	■	A
Mobility Super Attack (during mobility move)	X+R	■+R1	A+R
Dodge Attack	D-pad+Y,X	D-pad+▲,■	D-pad+Y,A
Dodge Super Attack	D-pad+Y,X+R	D-pad+▲,■+R1	D-pad+Y,A+R
Air Tackle (during flight or jump)	B	●	X
Super Air Tackle (during flight or jump)	B+R	●+R1	X+R
Block	Y	▲	Y
Super Block (invincible)	Y+R	▲+R1	Y+R
Finishing Move (when opponent in Danger Mode)	B+R	●+R1	X+R

*Controls for Wall Hang are character dependant. Wolverine, Elektra, Fault Zone, and Paragon use the R button to stick to walls. Spider-Man and Venom use the L button to stick to walls.

NOTE

You can recharge your superpower meter by standing still and holding the superpower button.

Combo List

This list of potential combinations is for reference across all characters. Please note that not all combos are available to all characters.

COMBINATIONS	Xbox			
ATTACK COMBOS	*Attack 1*	*Attack 2*	*Attack 3*	*Attack 4*
Regular Combo 1	X	X	X	Special: X or X+R for characters able to perform 4-hit combos
Regular Combo 2	X	X	X+R	
Regular Combo 3	X	X+R	X	
Regular Combo 4	X	X+R	X+R	
SUPER ATTACK COMBOS	*Attack 1*	*Attack 2*	*Attack 3*	*Attack 4*
Super Combo 1	X+R	X+R	X+R	Special: X or X+8 for characters able to perform 4-hit combos
Super Combo 2	X+R	X+R	X	
Super Combo 3	X+R	X	X+R	
Super Combo 4	X+R	X	X	
FAR ATTACKS	*Attack 1*	*Attack 2*		
Regular Far Combo	X	X or X+R		
Super Far Combo	X	X or X+R		
AIR ATTACK COMBOS	*Attack 1*	*Attack 2*		
Regular Air Combo	A,X	X		
RISING COMBOS (FROM PRONE)	*Attack 1*	*Attack 2*		
Rising Attack Combo	X	A,X		
Rising Super Attack Combo	X	A,X+R		
Rising Air Tackle	X	A,B		
Rising Super Air Tackle	X	A,B+R		
Super Rising Attack Combo	X+R	A,X		
Super Rising Super Attack Combo	X+R	A,X+R		
Super Rising Air Tackle	X+R	A,B		
Super Rising Super Air Tackle	X+R	A,B+R		
DODGING COMBOS	*Move 1*	*Attack 1*		
Dodging Jump Attack	D-pad+Y	A,X		
Dodging Super Jump Attack	D-pad+Y	A,X+R		
Dodging Air Tackle	D-pad+Y	A,B		
Dodging Super Air Tackle	D-pad+Y	A,B+R		

PlayStation 2

Attack 1	Attack 2	Attack 3	Attack 4
■	■	■	Special: ■ or ■+[R1] for characters able to perform 4-hit combos
■	■	■+[R1]	
■	■+[R1]	■	
■	■+[R1]	■+[R1]	

Attack 1	Attack 2	Attack 3	Attack 4
■+[R1]	■+[R1]	■+[R1]	Special: ■ or ■+[R1] for characters able to perform 4-hit combos
■+[R1]	■+[R1]	■	
■+[R1]	■	■+[R1]	
■+[R1]	■	■	

Attack 1	Attack 2
■	■ or ■+[R1]
■	■ or ■+[R1]

Attack 1	Attack 2
U,■	■

Attack 1	Attack 2
■	×,■
■	×,■+[R1]
■	×,●
■	×,●+[R1]
■+[R1]	×,P
■+[R1]	×,■+[R1]
■+[R1]	×,●
■+[R1]	×,■+[R1]

Move 1	Attack 1
D-pad+▲	×,■
D-pad+▲	×,■+[R1]
D-pad+▲	×,●
D-pad+▲	×,●+[R1]

GameCube

Attack 1	Attack 2	Attack 3	Attack 4
Ⓐ	Ⓐ	Ⓐ	Special: Ⓐ or Ⓐ+[R] for characters able to perform 4-hit combos
Ⓐ	Ⓐ	Ⓐ+[R]	
Ⓐ	Ⓐ+[R]	Ⓐ	
Ⓐ	Ⓐ+[R]	Ⓐ+[R]	

Attack 1	Attack 2	Attack 3	Attack 4
Ⓐ+[R]	Ⓐ+[R]	Ⓐ+[R]	Special: Ⓐ or Ⓐ+[R] for characters able to perform 4-hit combos
Ⓐ+[R]	Ⓐ+[R]	Ⓐ	
Ⓐ+[R]	Ⓐ	Ⓐ+[R]	
Ⓐ+[R]	Ⓐ	Ⓐ	

Attack 1	Attack 2
Ⓐ	Ⓐ or Ⓐ+[R]
Ⓐ	Ⓐ or Ⓐ+[R]

Attack 1	Attack 2
Ⓑ,Ⓐ	Ⓐ

Attack 1	Attack 2
Ⓐ	Ⓑ,Ⓐ
Ⓐ	Ⓑ,Ⓐ+[R]
Ⓐ	Ⓑ,Ⓧ
Ⓐ	Ⓑ,Ⓧ+[R]
Ⓐ+[R]	Ⓑ,Ⓐ
Ⓐ+[R]	Ⓑ,Ⓐ+[R]
Ⓐ+[R]	Ⓑ,Ⓧ
Ⓐ+[R]	Ⓑ,Ⓧ+[R]

Move 1	Attack 1
D-pad+Ⓨ	Ⓑ,Ⓐ
D-pad+Ⓨ	Ⓑ,Ⓐ+[R]
D-pad+Ⓨ	Ⓑ,Ⓧ
D-pad+Ⓨ	Ⓑ,Ⓧ+[R]

Marvel Heroes and the Imperfects

introduction

Now down to the nitty-gritty. Here we cover characters and give you the 411 on their fighting styles, special moves, and tactics for how to beat their AI.

Much of the following material is self-explanatory, however a few items are noteworthy: power grid, power summary boxes, special moves, critical hits, and fighting-against strategies.

The power grid is a graphical representation of any given character's attributes. These attributes are in tune with their real-world fiction, taken right from the Marvel Universe, and have been more or less incorporated into the game. But that's as far as it goes. Don't spend too much time comparing and analyzing one person's power grid to the next, as the gameplay implications are limited.

The power summary boxes give a brief outline of what that character is all about. Most of the items described are straightforward, with the exception of combat and defensive strategies. Combat strategy is a rough guide to how that character fights, a generalization combined from both fiction and gameplay. Defensive strategy is much the same, with hints about a character's strength and mobility with how he or she defends against various attacks. For example, a hero with high mobility is more likely to dodge than block, while a character with high energy reserves will super block more frequently than others.

The special moves tables show the techniques that are characteristically unique to that individual—despite the fact that general move types are carried out exactly the same way regardless of who you're controlling. For instance, a super mobility attack with Storm is exactly the same button sequence as a super mobility attack with Hazmat. Thanks to the universal control system, no overly complicated button presses are required to enact the dramatic moves.

Juggles are very important techniques to master. Here we list every move a character is able to execute that knocks their opponent into the air for follow-up attacks. Most commonly, juggles are used to set up your opponents for air combos or air tackles. Using this tactic, it's possible to get more than five moves linked together for some characters—and that means excessive damage.

The critical hits table gives a character's high-damage attacks so you just have to focus on laying the beats down on your opponents. These are not *all* of a character's moves. Learn the others from the move key in "The Basics" section.

The "fighting-against" strategies box is a summary of the AI version of the respective character. It includes a semi-ranked list of the most common attacks they use against you, and also continues with some tactics on how to use specific strategies to beat them. These strategies can also be applied to human-controlled characters in Versus mode.

introduction
the basics
marvel heroes
the imperfects
story mode
arenas
online play
cheats and rewards

marvel heroes

Daredevil

Intro

He dwells in a world of eternal night—but the blackness is filled with sounds and scents, tastes and textures most men cannot perceive. Although attorney Matt Murdock is blind, his other four senses function with superhuman sharpness. He stalks the streets at night, a relentless avenger of justice: Daredevil, the Man Without Fear.

Profile

Real Name:	Matthew Michael Murdock
Occupation:	Adventurer
Group Affiliation:	None
Base of Operations:	New York
Height:	6'
Weight:	200 lbs.
Eye Color:	Blue
Hair Color:	Red

Power Grid

- Intelligence
- Strength
- Speed
- Durability
- Energy Projection
- Fighting Skills

Tip: Daredevil can throw opponents from a distance by pushing Super and Throw. Use this tactic to toss your opponent out of the arena.

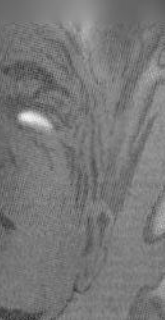

POWER SUMMARY

SUMMARY ITEM	DESCRIPTION
Strengths	Swinging, long-range attacks, long-range throws, wall running
Weaknesses	None
Environmental Advantages	Can use walls to his advantage in combination with mobility attacks; can recover from ring-out situations
Environmental Disadvantages	Electricity causes damage and stun
Combat Strategies	Swinging attacks, billy club attacks, wall attacks, dodging attacks, mobility attacks
Defensive Strategies	Dodging, redirecting, normal block, super block

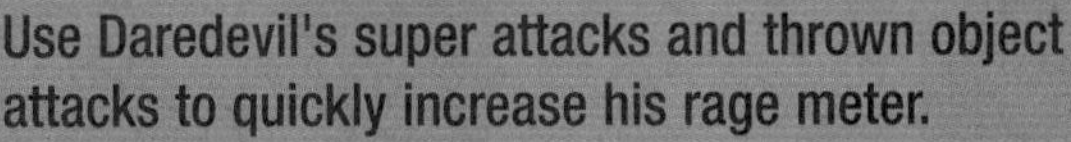

TIP

Use Daredevil's super attacks and thrown object attacks to quickly increase his rage meter.

SPECIAL MOVES, JUGGLES, AND CRITICAL HITS

SPECIAL MOVES

Move Type	*Move Name*	*Xbox*	*PS2/PSP*	*NGC*
Mobility Move	Wall Run	D-pad+(L)	D-pad+L1	D-pad+L
Mobility Move	Swinging	(L)	L1	L
Super Far Attack	Billy Club Boomerang	(X)+(R)	■+R1	(A)+R
Super Throw	Billy Club Throw	(B)+(R)	●+R1	(X)+R

CRITICAL HITS (HIGH-DAMAGE ATTACKS)

Attack Type	*Move Name*
Super Attack 3 (3rd move in combo)	Spinning Billy Club Smash
Super Far Attack	Billy Club Boomerang Throw
Super Throw	Billy Club Throw
Wall Run Super Attack	Grappling Hook Lasso Loop
Super Rising Attack	Uppercut Billy Stick
Mobility Regular Attack	Sliding Billy Club Uppercut
Dodging Super Attack	Billy Club Boomerang Throw
Finishing Move	Multi-arm Break

JUGGLING MOVES

Last Regular Attack	•
Last Super Attack	
Mobility Regular Attack	
Mobility Super Attack	•
Rising Attack	•
Rising Super Attack	
Dodge Regular Attack	•
Dodge Super Attack	

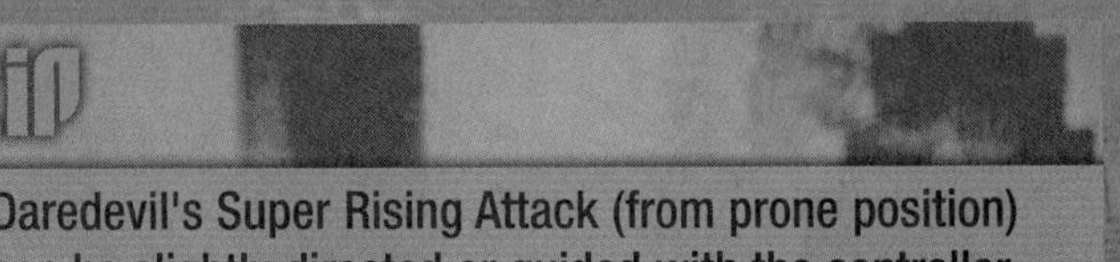

TIP

Daredevil's Super Rising Attack (from prone position) can be slightly directed or guided with the controller. So if Daredevil misses the opponent when the club goes out, he can steer it to hit the opponent when it comes back to him.

fighting-against strategies

Daredevil's fighting style is all about mobility: speed and agility mixed with excellent technical martial arts and acrobatic abilities. The advantage he gets from such high mobility comes in several forms, but he really is an exceptionally well-rounded fighter. Expect to see much of these elements below when fighting an AI Daredevil:

1. Swinging Attacks
2. Billy Club Attacks
3. Wall Attacks
4. Dodging Attacks

Here are a few tips to help keep Daredevil's billy clubs from cracking off your skull:

tactics

- The middle ground belongs to Daredevil due to his high mobility. Either stay out of range and keep hitting him with longer-range attacks than his, or get in close for some intense hand-to-hand combat action. In the middle, he'll dance circles around you.
- Daredevil's rage mode lasts almost as long as Wolverine's. Avoid him if you can when he's in this state, because all of his super (billy club) attacks pack quite a punch.
- Many of his attacks are dodging and mobility attacks (walls, swinging, and far attacks) to mix it up and confuse you. He changes direction easily using dodging attacks, so it can be difficult to pin him down in one spot for too long.
- Keep him off the walls and out of the air by hurling weapons, objects, or ranged attacks at him.
- Daredevil tries to dodge more than block, so if you're fast you can usually nail him with light thrown objects.
- Be cautious of his occasional rising attacks. They can catch you off guard easily and set him up for some brutal follow-up combinations.

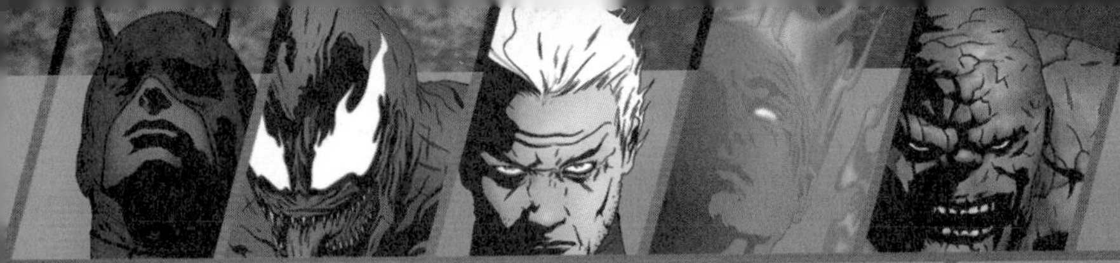

HISTORY

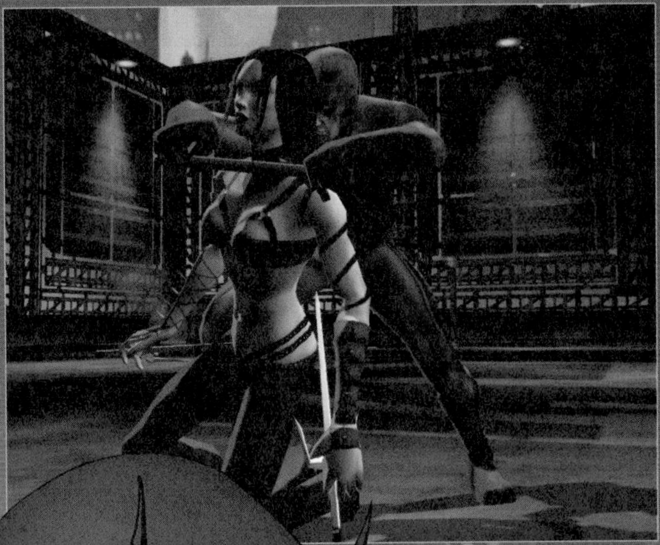

The son of a small-time boxer, Matt Murdock was taught by his father that fighting was not the answer to life's problems. As raised by his father, Matt was selflessly noble. This was never more apparent than when he pushed an elderly man out of the path of a runaway truck. Matt's kindness was cruelly repaid by fate when radioactive waste from the vehicle's payload splashed onto his eyes, blinding him.

Devastated at first by his apparent handicap, Matt slowly came to realize that the accident had radically augmented his ability to perceive the world around him. His vision was gone, but the radioactivity had heightened his other senses to a superhuman degree.

Unable to adjust to his overdeveloped senses, the terrified Matt eventually came under the tutelage of the blind martial-arts master Stick. A stern, unrelenting taskmaster, Stick educated Matt in both the spiritual and physical aspects of the martial arts, refusing to let him think of himself as a helpless victim. Matt emerged as an Olympic-class gymnast and formidable hand-to-hand combatant.

Matt's pain and guilt over the losses in his life have replaced his earlier motivations, fueling his battles as Daredevil long after any reasonable man would have quit the fight. In the wake of so many deaths, Matt's suffering and grief are his only constant companions. Night after night, he struggles to safeguard Hell's Kitchen—seeking absolution and forgiveness from those who have long since lost the ability to clear his conscience.

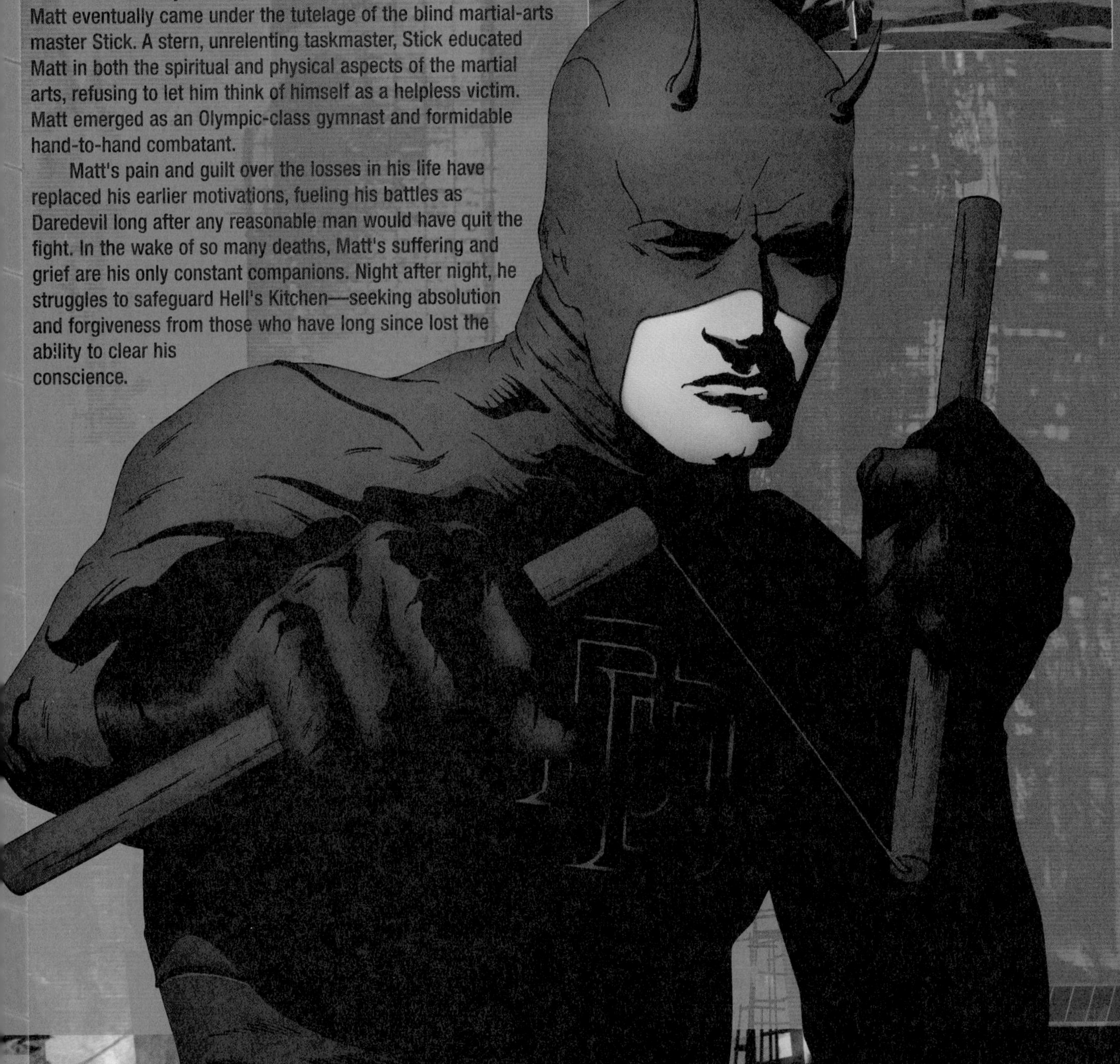

MARVEL HEROES

ELEKTRA

INTRO

The world's most dangerous assassin, Elektra remains a mystery, a shadow—until she chooses to reveal herself. Trained as a ninja, loyal to no one, she sells her amazing abilities and her mastery of the deadly sai to the highest bidder.

PROFILE

REAL NAME:	Elektra Natchios
OCCUPATION:	Adventurer
GROUP AFFILIATION:	None
BASE OF OPERATIONS:	New York
HEIGHT:	5' 9"
WEIGHT:	130 lbs.
EYE COLOR:	Blue-Black
HAIR COLOR:	Black

POWER GRID

Attribute	Rating (of 7)
INTELLIGENCE	3
STRENGTH	2
SPEED	2
DURABILITY	3
ENERGY PROJECTION	1
FIGHTING SKILLS	6

TIP

If you quickly push Jump, then Attack, you can knock your opponent into the air for a quick Air Combo (takes some practice).

Power Summary

SUMMARY ITEM	DESCRIPTION
Strengths	Wall-runner, wall-climber, long-range attacks, 4-hit combos
Weaknesses	None
Environmental Advantages	Can aggressively use walls to her advantage
Environmental Disadvantages	Electricity causes damage and stun, can't recover from ring-out situations
Combat Strategies	Mobility attacks, super combo attacks, wall attacks, ranged attacks
Defensive Strategies	Dodging, redirecting, super blocking, normal blocking

Tip

Elektra is one of the only characters able to execute four-hit combos.

Special Moves, Juggles, and Critical Hits

SPECIAL MOVES

Move Type	*Move Name*	*Xbox*	*PS2/PSP*	*NGC*
Mobility Move	Wall Run	D-pad+L	D-pad+L1	D-pad+L
Mobility Move	Wall Hang	D-pad+L+R	D-pad+L1+R1	D-pad+L+R
Super Far Attack	Double Kunai Throw	X+R	■+R1	A+R

CRITICAL HITS (HIGH-DAMAGE ATTACKS)

Attack Type	*Move Name*
Super Attack 1	Left Uppercut Twirling Sai
Super Attack 2	Right Hook Twirling Sai
Super Attack 3	Double Twirling Sai Stab
Super Attack 4	360 Angled Spinning Slash
Super Throw	Sai Hook Monkeyflip Toss
Wall Run Regular Attack	Flying Sidekick
Wall Run Super Attack	Double Sai Dive
Super Rising Attack	Rising Kunai Throw
Dodge Super Attack	Single Kunai Throw
Finishing Move	Stab Kick Sai Kick Throw

JUGGLING MOVES

Last Regular Attack	•
Last Super Attack	
Mobility Regular Attack	
Mobility Super Attack	
Rising Attack	•
Rising Super Attack	
Dodge Regular Attack	•
Dodge Super Attack	

Tip

Use object and mobility attacks to increase Elektra's rage meter the fastest.

fighting-against strategies

Elektra is the perfect assassin—martial artist, ninja, hero. Her dark past is fraught with conflict, but when it comes to a fight, she is single-minded. If she's focused on you, bust out the first aid kit because there's going to be trouble! Here are some tendencies you'll see when fighting an AI Elektra:

1. Melee Attacks Combos
2. Mobility Attacks
3. Dodging Attacks
4. Super Attack Combos
5. Air Tackles

tactics

When you're battling an assassin trained by the Hand, you must know this isn't going to be a walk in the park. Where Elektra lacks in power, she makes up for twofold in deadly precision—many of her techniques are high-damage attacks because she knows not just how to fight but how to kill. Use the following tactics when you face the lethal assassin Elektra:

- Elektra is dangerous at a distance with her double kunai throw. Both sais shoot out very quickly; find some cover until she's changed tactics.
- Make her expend her SP meter before moving in—ideally by forcing her to super block trying to deflect a thrown object. Her regular attacks are not as dangerous as her super attacks.
- Considering Elektra is so dangerous with her super moves, keep her from reaching rage mode if possible. Even 20 seconds of a raging Elektra is enough to vanquish most foes.
- Stay on the ground—Elektra is quite skilled at grabbing opponents out of the air and slamming them to the ground. Her air tackles are not that powerful, but from there she can launch more fatal combo attacks.
- She's highly mobile and uses walls often to her advantage. If she's going for the wall it helps to be either right below her or far enough away to avoid her wall attacks.
- Elektra attempts dodging more than she does blocking. Anticipate her direction changes and use them against her.
- When she's low on SP and it's safe to engage her in hand-to-hand combat, get right in close to lay on the super throws. Elektra is not very resilient to this kind of damage.
- Throw objects at her to whittle down her health and stamina. At a distance she throws her sais, which are very quick across the arena. But if you beat her to the punch, the hurled objects will do some sweet damage.

HISTORY

Elektra is the daughter is a powerful Greek diplomat. When her father was accidentally killed during a hostage crisis, Elektra was emotionally shattered and withdrew from the civilized world. Alone and angry, she set out in search of meaning and purpose, guidance and training. Elektra's quest led her abroad, where she studied the martial arts with a sensei in Japan.

In search of a true and total peace of spirit, Elektra later joined the noble order of warriors led by Stick. She honed her fighting skills to the peak of human perfection, but Stick saw that Elektra was filled with pain over her father's death and with hatred for the world she blamed for it. He expelled her from his order, and she found herself alone once again.

Still determined to prove herself to Stick, Elektra infiltrated the Hand, a cult of ninjas devoted to assassination and domination by fear, intending to subvert their activities. The Hand trained and guided her, twisting her soul, but Elektra never turned completely. Eventually, she rebelled against the Hand and fled Japan.

Following an epic confrontation with Bullseye that left both combatants bloodied and battered, Bullseye impaled Elektra on her own sai. Elektra died in Daredevil's arms. Brought back to life through a mystical ceremony, Elektra left Daredevil's side, determined to find her own place in the world.

marvel heroes

human torch

intro

Mutagenically transformed by cosmic rays into the heroic Human Torch, Johnny Storm is the hothead of the Fantastic Four. Able to envelop himself in fiery plasma, the Human Torch has the ability to fly and project fire blasts from his hands.

profile

real name:	Jonathan Storm
occupation:	Adventurer
group affiliation:	Fantastic Four
base of operations:	New York
height:	5' 10"
weight:	170 lbs.
eye color:	Blue
hair color:	Blond

power grid

Attribute	Rating (of 7)
intelligence	2
strength	2
speed	5
durability	2
energy projection	5
fighting skills	3

POWER SUMMARY

SUMMARY ITEM	DESCRIPTION
Strengths	Flier, fast mobility in air, ranged attacks, nearly immune to fire attacks
Weaknesses	None
Environmental Advantages	Can recover from ring-out situations
Environmental Disadvantages	None
Combat Strategies	Mobility, super far attacks (fireball), super combo attacks
Defensive Strategies	Dodging, normal blocking, super blocking, redirecting

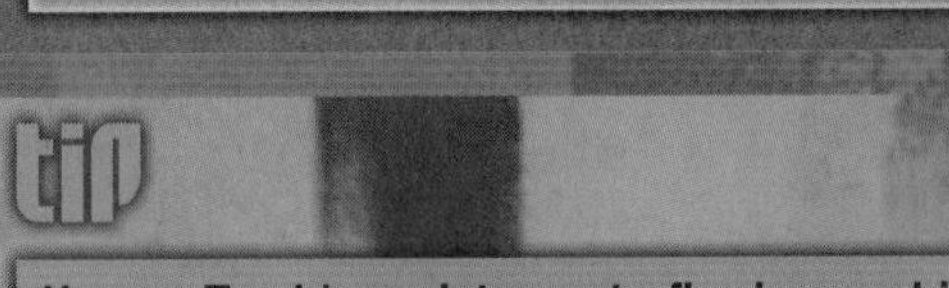

TIP

Human Torch's resistance to fire is very high. If his own attack gets reflected back to him he only takes negligible damage.

SPECIAL MOVES, JUGGLES, AND CRITICAL HITS

SPECIAL MOVES

Move Type	*Move Name*	*Xbox*	*PS2/PSP*	*NGC*
Mobility Move	Fly	L	L1	→
Mobility Move	Double-Fisted Air Ram Attack	X	■	↙
Super Far Attack	Fireball	X+R	■+R1	↙+↖
Super Dodging Attack	Fireball Blast	D-pad+Y,X+R	D-pad+▲,■+R1	D-pad+←,↙+↖

CRITICAL HITS (HIGH-DAMAGE ATTACKS)

Attack Type	*Move Name*
Super Attack 3	2-Hand Palm Thrust
Super Attack Far	Fireball
Super Throw	Fire Blast Throw
Super Rising Attack	Rising Fireball Blast
Dodge Super Attack	Fireball Blast
Finishing Move	Immolation

JUGGLING MOVES

Last Regular Attack	•
Last Super Attack	
Mobility Regular Attack	
Mobility Super Attack	
Rising Attack	•
Rising Super Attack	
Dodge Regular Attack	•
Dodge Super Attack	

TIP

Torch's rage period is quite short, approximately 10 seconds, so use it wisely! Super attacks are the best way to get him into rage mode.

Fighting-Against Strategies

The Human Torch is an extremely straightforward fighter—very linear in style. He hits and runs in and out with speed and grace; there are few extraneous moves in his repertoire. When he attacks, anticipate him to come in hard and fast, commonly with a double-fisted air ram. Expect these elements when fighting an AI Human Torch:

1. Super Far Attacks (air)
2. Ranged Attacks (fireballs)
3. Super Combo Attacks
4. Air Combos
5. Air Tackles

Here are a few tips to keep you from being burned by the Human Torch:

Tactics

- Better fighters should get in close and take the fight to him. In hand-to-hand combat the Torch is not much of a threat, but expect a few fiery bursts now and again.
- Once he's knocked down, get a cheap shot in and back off. His rising super attack is a high-damage technique and can take you off your feet.
- Don't worry too much about Torch's rage mode; it's very short lived. Hit him hard and don't let him use it to his advantage.
- Let him come to you. Torch's high mobility makes chasing him around something like trying to catch a zippy little firefly with chopsticks. Use a self-defense style: wait for him to attack you and then beat him down!
- Use your blocks and super blocks as often as possible against his ranged attacks.
- Beware the fireball blast near ring-out areas—it knocks you up and back through the air.
- Air tackles work wonders against the Torch, as he spends so much time flying. Bring him back down to Earth!

history

Johnny Storm was a passenger on the Fantastic Four's fateful journey into space. Rather than being the preeminent experience of Johnny's young life, the trip proved to be a disaster. In space, the starship unexpectedly encountered intense radiation, which mutagenically altered the bodies of all four crew members.

Having acquired the ability to emit and envelop himself in fiery plasma, Johnny jumped at the promise of adventure when Reed suggested they use their unique powers for humanity's benefit. Upon graduation from high school, Johnny moved to the team's Baxter Building headquarters in New York City.

Like any other family, the members of the Fantastic Four have endured their share of hardships, always remaining together because of their love for one another, not out of necessity. The baby of the bunch, the Torch has demonstrated a talent for tormenting the Thing. Ben and Johnny may bicker like brothers, but each is extremely protective of the other.

Immature and prone to distraction in other areas, Johnny nonetheless endeavors to live up to his heroic responsibilities—when he's not jet-setting in one of his souped-up hot rods, wooing women with his boyish good looks and natural charm, or attempting to kick start his acting career. But no matter how many times they tell him to grow up, the Torch is in no great hurry to become an adult. Impetuous and hotheaded, he often charges headlong into the breach, leaving Mr. Fantastic and Invisible Woman to pick up the pieces in his wake—and the Thing to pull his fat out of the fire.

MARVEL HEROES

IRON MAN

INTRO

Gravely injured by an act of industrial sabotage, billionaire genius Tony Stark saved his own life by designing a life-sustaining shell—the high-tech armor that is the invincible Iron Man.

PROFILE

Real Name:	Anthony Stark
Occupation:	Billionaire Industrialist
Group Affiliation:	Avengers
Base of Operations:	New York
Height:	6' 1"
Weight:	225 lbs.
Eye Color:	Blue
Hair Color:	Black

POWER GRID

Intelligence
Strength
Speed
Durability
Energy Projection
Fighting Skills

POWER SUMMARY

SUMMARY ITEM	DESCRIPTION
Strengths	Flier, long-range attacks
Weaknesses	Large superpower consumption
Environmental Advantages	Acid causes little to no damage, minimal damage from smashing through objects, can recover from ring-out situations
Environmental Disadvantages	Electricity causes damage and stun
Combat Strategies	Super far attacks (ranged and flying), throwing objects and weapons
Defensive Strategies	Normal blocking, super blocking, dodging, redirecting

TIP

Mobility and object attacks increase Iron Man's rage meter the fastest. Use rage mode efficiently because the duration is limited to near 10 seconds.

SPECIAL MOVES, JUGGLES, AND CRITICAL HITS

SPECIAL MOVES

Move Type	*Move Name*	*Xbox*	*PS2/PSP*	*NGC*
Mobility Move	Flying	L	L1	L
Mobility Attack	Shoulder Air Ram	X	■	A
Mobility Super Attack	Homing Missile	X+R	■+R1	A+R
Super Far Attack	Repulsor Rays	X+R	■+R1	A+R
Dodge Super Attack	Repulsor Blast	D-pad+Y, X+R	D-pad+▲, ■+R1	D-pad+Y, A+R

CRITICAL HITS (HIGH-DAMAGE ATTACKS)

Attack Type	*Move Name*
Super Attack 2	1-Hand Palm Thrust
Super Attack 3	Repulsor Ray
Super Attack Far	Repulsor Ray
Super Throw	Repulsor Blast to Face
Jump Super Attack	Repulsor Ray
Super Attack Stomp	Kneeling Repulsor Ray
Super Rising Attack	Upward Repulsor Ray
Dodge Super Attack	Repulsor Blast
Super Air Tackle	Repulsor Blast into Ground
Finishing Move	Uni-Beam

JUGGLING MOVES

Move	
Last Regular Attack	•
Last Super Attack	
Mobility Regular Attack	
Mobility Super Attack	
Rising Attack	•
Rising Super Attack	
Dodge Regular Attack	•
Dodge Super Attack	

fighting-against strategies

Iron Man is something of a modern-day knight, not without his dark secrets, but somewhat more noble than others. His fighting style focuses on the extraordinary strength and energy projection of his armor. Don't expect a lot of flashy moves, but you can expect him to make the most of his environment. Here are a few common elements you'll see when fighting an AI Iron Man:

1. Ranged Attacks (repulsors)
2. Throwing Objects
3. Mobility Attacks (flying)
4. Super Attack Combos

Here are a few tips and tricks to assist your cause against the noble Iron Man:

tactics

- Know your environments well; Iron Man makes full use of everything around him and he can pick up any class object to hurl at you.
- Air tackles work well against him, as he spends a lot of time flying.
- Due to his armor, Iron Man won't commonly block or dodge—he's not overly concerned with many physical attacks.
- Watch his SP meter; using his suit requires giga-joules of energy. Play cat and mouse with him until his SP is low and then go after him relentlessly. If he can't execute his mobility or super attacks, you'll have a brief advantage.
- Iron Man is still susceptible to ring outs. Because his suit requires so much power, if he's blown far enough over the edge he may not have enough to get back into the arena.

history

The son of a wealthy industrialist, Tony Stark was an inventive mechanical engineering prodigy. He inherited his father's business at age 21, transforming the company, Stark International, into one of the world's leading weapons manufacturers. While field-testing a suit of battle armor in Asia that would enhance a soldier's combat capabilities, Stark was struck in the chest by a piece of shrapnel and taken prisoner by the warlord Wong-Chu. He was ordered to create a weapon of mass destruction.

Stark began work on a modified exoskeleton equipped with heavy weaponry and donned the suit in an attempt to escape captivity. Overcoming the warlord's forces, Stark returned to America and redesigned the suit. Inventing the cover story that Iron Man was his bodyguard, he embarked on a double life as a billionaire industrialist and costumed adventurer.

At first little more than a glorified security guard, Iron Man's early opponents included industrial spies and foreign agents, all intent on stealing Stark's defense and military secrets. Over time, Stark ceased simply protecting his own interests. He expanded the scope of his activities to include threats to national and international security. Iron Man even helped found the Avengers, and Stark became the team's corporate sponsor.

As Iron Man's opponents and needs have changed, so has the hero's armor. Stark has grown to feel more responsible for the use of his technology throughout the world. He has realized that by and large, his legacy is one of destruction and warfare as nations employ his early inventions to oppress and kill. Stark Enterprises broke off its relationship with the U.S. government, refusing to manufacture any weapons and focusing instead on technology that would enhance human life.

Magneto

Intro

The self-appointed Master of Magnetism has dedicated his life to the advancement of *Homo superior*, even if he must bring about humanity's downfall to ensure the ascendance of mutantkind. Arguably the most powerful man on earth, Magneto believes that mutants represent the next step in evolution.

Profile

Real Name:	Erik Magnus Lensherr
Occupation:	Conqueror
Group Affiliation:	Brotherhood of Mutants
Base of Operations:	Genosha
Height:	6' 2"
Weight:	190 lbs.
Eye Color:	Bluish-gray
Hair Color:	Silver

Power Grid

Attribute	Rating (of 7)
Intelligence	5
Strength	2
Speed	5
Durability	6
Energy Projection	5
Fighting Skills	3

POWER SUMMARY

SUMMARY ITEM	DESCRIPTION
Strengths	Flier, ranged attacks
Weaknesses	Limited melee skills, 2-hit combos only
Environmental Advantages	Can recover from ring-out situations
Environmental Disadvantages	None
Combat Strategies	Super far attacks (air and ground), super combo attacks
Defensive Strategies	Super block, dodging, normal block, redirecting

TIP

Mobility and object attacks increase Iron Man's rage meter the fastest. Use rage mode efficiently because the duration is limited to near 10 seconds.

SPECIAL MOVES, JUGGLES, AND CRITICAL HITS

SPECIAL MOVES

Move Type	*Move Name*	*Xbox*	*PS2/PSP*	*NGC*
Mobility Move	Fly	L	L1	L
Super Attack Far	Magnetic Projectile Attack	X+R	■+R1	A+R
Super Throw	Magnetic Throw (both people and objects)	B+R	●+R1	X+R

CRITICAL HITS (HIGH-DAMAGE ATTACKS)

Attack Type	*Move Name*
Super Attack 1	Left-Handed Palm Thrust
Super Attack 2	2-Handed Palm Thrust
Super Attack Far	Projectile Attack
Super Throw	Object Throw
Super Rising Attack	Levitate and Blast
Dodge Super Attack	Projectile Attack
Finishing Move	Metal Ballistics

JUGGLING MOVES

Move	
Last Regular Attack	
Last Super Attack	•
Mobility Regular Attack	
Mobility Super Attack	
Rising Attack	•
Rising Super Attack	
Dodge Regular Attack	•
Dodge Super Attack	

TIP

Magneto can grab props from a distance, but unlike other characters with the same ability (i.e., Spider-Man), he can throw the prop at his enemy while the prop is flying toward him by pressing the attack button.

fighting-against strategies

Hand-to-hand combat is for fools, at least in the eyes of the Master of Magnetism. He would much rather swat you like a fly with a 10-ton radio tower or completely immobilize you using nothing but the iron in your blood. The environment is his weapon of choice, and he'll hit you with everything you see around you. Here are the most common elements you'll see when fighting an AI Magneto:

1. Super Throws (objects)
2. Super Throws (YOU!)
3. Super Far Attacks (magnetic projectiles)
4. Super Combo Attacks

Use these tactics to keep Magneto from crushing you like a tin can:

tactics

- Destroy all the props in the arena—the less he has to hurl at you the better!
- Hand-to-hand combat is most effective; get in close and kick butt. When it comes down to the punch, most fighters are better in close than silvery haired Mr. Lensherr.
- Magneto has a very fast dodge; if he is throwing dodging attacks as follow-ups it will be hard to pin him down. It's better to back off and regroup, then come at him again.
- He super blocks more often than most opponents because his SP recharges quite quickly—basically, he can afford to. Bait him into using his super block by throwing objects or firing ranged attacks at him. When his meter runs short, hit him with everything you've got.
- Beware of Magneto's super rising attack, which is a heavy hitter—if you're going in to lay the boots to him while he's down, be prepared for a nasty surprise.
- Air maneuvers sometimes go unnoticed around him, but rest assured that Magneto does have a powerful super air tackle that he will use in a pinch. If you're not a flier, it's better to keep Magneto on the ground—don't try to compete with him on his own terms by jumping around after him.

HISTORY

Long before he learned of his mutant powers, Magneto felt the bitter sting of discrimination. He spent his youth interred at the Nazi death camp in Auschwitz, Poland, and was the only member of his family to survive the Holocaust. To Magnus, this experience bluntly and irrevocably demonstrated mankind's potential for inhumanity.

Years later, he befriended Charles Xavier, a young mutant telepath. Xavier held fast to his optimistic belief that *Homo sapiens* and *Homo superior* could coexist, while Magnus foresaw mutants as the next minority to be persecuted for their differences. Magnus desperately tried to share his friend's hope, but was unwilling to stand by, powerless, while history repeated itself.

Now calling himself Magneto, Magnus became determined to conquer the human race and thus prevent the oppression of his kind. Whatever doubts surround the Master of Magnetism, one fact is certain: Magneto is a survivor. As he lived through the Holocaust, he will return to prevent the persecution of his people. Magneto has dedicated his life to the advancement of mutantkind, even if he must bring about humanity's downfall to ensure the ascendance of *Homo superior*. Arguably the most powerful being on Earth, Magneto believes mutants represent the next step in human evolution, and he's grown weary of waiting for *Homo sapiens* to cede control of the planet.

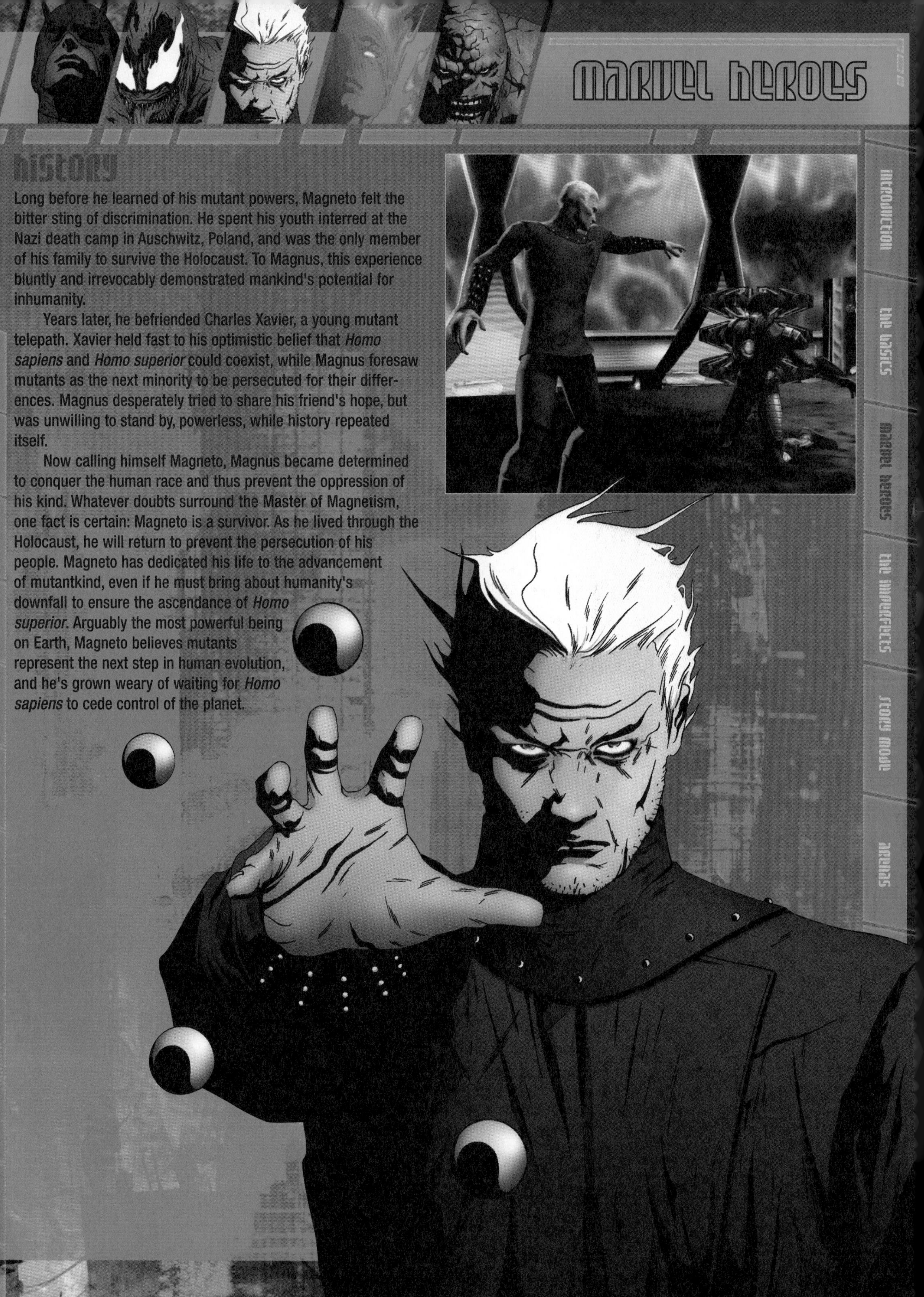

MARVEL HEROES

SPIDER-MAN

INTRO

The bite of an irradiated spider granted high-school student Peter Parker incredible, arachnid-like powers. When a burglar killed his beloved Uncle Ben, a grief-stricken Peter vowed to use his amazing abilities to protect his fellow man. He had learned an invaluable lesson: With great power, there must also come great responsibility.

PROFILE

REAL NAME:	Peter Parker
OCCUPATION:	Adventurer
GROUP AFFILIATION:	None
BASE OF OPERATIONS:	New York
HEIGHT:	5' 10"
WEIGHT:	165 lbs.
EYE COLOR:	Brown
HAIR COLOR:	Brown

POWER GRID

INTELLIGENCE
STRENGTH
SPEED
DURABILITY
ENERGY PROJECTION
FIGHTING SKILLS

TIP Spider-Man can grab objects from a distance by pushing Super and Throw together while targeting the item with the analog stick or D-pad.

introduction | the basics | marvel heroes | the imperfects | story mode | arenas | online play | cheats and rewards

POWER SUMMARY

SUMMARY ITEM	DESCRIPTION
Strengths	Long-range attacks, swinging, wall climbing, long-range throws, 4-hit combos
Weaknesses	None
Environmental Advantages	Can effectively use walls to his advantage, can recover from ring-out situations
Environmental Disadvantages	Electricity causes damage and stun
Combat Strategies	Swinging attacks, wall attacks, super far attacks, dodging attacks
Defensive Strategies	Dodging, redirecting, normal blocking, super blocking

Use Spider-Man's mobility attacks to quickly raise his rage meter.

SPECIAL MOVES, JUGGLES, AND CRITICAL HITS

SPECIAL MOVES

Move Type	*Move Name*	*Xbox*	*PS2/PSP*	*NGC*
Mobility Move (air)	Swinging	L	L1	L
Mobility Move (ground)	Zipline	L	L1	L
Mobility Move	Wall Climb	D-pad+L+R	D-pad+L1+R1	D-pad+L+R
Super Far Attack	Web Bullets	X+R	■+R1	A+R
Super Throw (Objects)	Zipline Grab	B+R	●+R1	X+R

CRITICAL HITS (HIGH-DAMAGE ATTACKS)

Attack Type	*Move Name*
Super Attack 4	Backflip Swing Double Kick
Super Attack Far	Web Bullets
Super Throw	Web Pull to Whiplash
Super Rising Attack	Web Bullet Kipup
Mobility Regular Attack	Double Kick
Mobility Super Attack	Web Bullets
Dodge Super Attack	Web Bullets
Finishing Move	Web Punches

JUGGLING MOVES

Last Regular Attack	•
Last Super Attack	
Mobility Regular Attack	
Mobility Super Attack	
Rising Attack	•
Rising Super Attack	
Dodge Regular Attack	•
Dodge Super Attack	

Spider-Man can tumble forward and backward quickly by holding Block, and rapidly tapping the analog stick or D-pad forward or backward.

TIP

Spider-Man can throw opponents from a distance by pushing Super and Throw together. This is a great way to catch an opponent off guard and throw him over the edge for a ring out.

fighting-against strategies

Most people already have a good idea of Spider-Man's fighting style—hard punches, web slinging, dodging blows, and a good dose of acrobatics. He's highly mobile and plays an excellent game of hit and run. That's exactly what you can expect when fighting an AI Spider-Man:

1. Swinging Attacks
2. Wall Attacks
3. Super Far Attacks
4. Dodging Attacks

To avoid becoming the proverbial fly in the spider's web, use these following techniques:

tactics

- Most of the time, Spidey can be counted on to do two things: attack with ranged or mobility attacks, and dodge whatever you throw at him. Slightly less frequently he uses jump attacks and tries redirecting your attacks. Only after his mobility and ranged attacks have whittled you down will he move in to follow up with melee (regular) and super combo attacks.
- Spidey doesn't spend much time using weapons and props to his advantage. That being said, his zipline ability is very useful for grabbing objects from a distance, and in a pinch he'll get hold of something quickly enough to hurl it your way.
- Walls are obviously his home-field advantage—don't spend much time underneath him when he's wall crawling.
- Air tackles are very effective against him because he enjoys swinging across most arenas: bring him back to ground level and crush him like a bug!
- Spidey's advantage is due to his mobility and ranged attacks; take these away and he's forced to fight in close quarters where you may find a much better advantage. Get in close with some super combos; super throws are good too, but remember he can recover from throws much more easily.

HISTORY

Orphaned at a young age, Peter Parker was raised by his Uncle Ben and Aunt May as if he were their own son. Exceptionally bright, Peter was also extremely shy. A social outcast with few friends, he sought solace in his studies. During a demonstration on radiation, a spider wandered into the radiation source and became irradiated. Dying, the spider fell on Peter's hand and bit him.

Leaving the TV studio following a taping, Peter chose to mind his own business when he encountered a burglar fleeing the scene of a robbery. Though he could have stopped the man, Peter allowed him to pass, arrogantly believing it was not his responsibility. Several days later, he returned home from a performance only to discover that an intruder had murdered his uncle.

Learning police had cornered the hoodlum in a nearby warehouse, a distraught Peter donned his Spider-Man costume and desperately rushed off to confront his uncle's killer. Employing his newfound abilities to capture the burglar, Peter realized the thief was the same criminal he had allowed to escape. Filled with remorse, Peter finally understood that with great power, there must also come great responsibility—and he vowed never to shirk his heroic responsibilities again.

Constantly balancing his responsibility as a hero with his personal life, and ever ready with a wisecrack to hide his personal struggles, Peter remains steadfast in living up to the responsibility that his great powers have thrust upon him, donning his Spider-Man costume for the good of all.

Marvel Heroes

Storm

Intro

Orphaned as a child, Ororo Munroe developed the power to command the forces of nature. As a member of the X-Men, she wields her unique genetic gifts to protect a world that hates and fears mutants.

Profile

Real Name:	Ororo Munroe
Occupation:	Adventurer
Group Affiliation:	X-Men
Base of Operations:	Mobile
Height:	5' 11"
Weight:	127 lbs.
Eye Color:	Blue
Hair Color:	White

Power Grid

Intelligence
Strength
Speed
Durability
Energy Projection
Fighting Skills

POWER SUMMARY

SUMMARY ITEM	DESCRIPTION
Strengths	Flier, long-range attacks (air and ground)
Weaknesses	None
Environmental Advantages	Nearly immune to electrical damage, can recover from ring-out situations
Environmental Disadvantages	None
Combat Strategies	Super far attacks (ground), super far attacks (air), super throws
Defensive Strategies	Normal block, dodging, super block, redirecting

TIP

Storm is slow to get into rage mode. Use any of her super attacks to boost the meter fastest.

SPECIAL MOVES, JUGGLES, AND CRITICAL HITS

SPECIAL MOVES

Move Type	*Move Name*	*Xbox*	*PS2/PSP*	*NGC*
Mobility Attack	Double-Fisted Air Ram	Ⓧ	■	Ⓐ
Mobility Super Attack	Ball Lightning	Ⓧ+Ⓡ	■+R1	Ⓐ+R
Super Far Attack	Lightning Strike	Ⓧ+Ⓡ	■+R1	Ⓐ+R

CRITICAL HITS (HIGH-DAMAGE ATTACKS)

Attack Type	*Move Name*
Super Attack 3	Double Palm Thrust
Super Attack Far	Lightning Strike
Super Throw	Wind Gust Throw
Super Rising Attack	Rising Lightning Strike
Dodge Super Attack	Lightning Strike
Finishing Move	Lightning Vortex

JUGGLING MOVES

Last Regular Attack	•
Last Super Attack	
Mobility Regular Attack	
Mobility Super Attack	
Rising Attack	•
Rising Super Attack	
Dodge Regular Attack	•
Dodge Super Attack	

Fighting-Against Strategies

She's a goddess; what more can we say? When you control the weather, your fighting style doesn't need much more to make you a dangerous opponent. Combined with her ranged attacks, Storm has a few solid melee combat techniques up her sleeves—and we mean sleeves metaphorically, have you seen her uniform? Here's a brief rundown of the most common techniques you can expect when fighting an AI Storm:

1. Ranged Attacks
2. Mobility Attacks
3. Super Throws

And here are some tactics you can use to keep from feeling like you've just been run over by a hurricane:

Tactics

- Storm is going to come at you hard with a good mix of ranged attacks and mobility attacks[EM]both of which mean a lot of electricity potentially coursing through your body!
- She is not the strongest character physically, so air tackles are not something she focuses on. Feel free to jump or fly around her often.
- As a flier, Storm is often easily caught by air tackles.
- Very rarely does she pick up a weapon or object to hurl at you: use everything on the map to your advantage.
- Storm can't block heavier objects, so the more you toss her way, the more likely it is that you'll knock her down to size. Barrels make great projectiles to knock her out of the sky.

history

As a child, a bomb destroyed Ororo's home during a Middle Eastern conflict. Ororo's parents were killed, but she survived, buried under tons of rubble near her mother's body. This traumatizing experience left Ororo with severe claustrophobia, which afflicts her still. Homeless and orphaned, she came under the tutelage of master thief Achmed el-Gibar. Ororo was his prize pupil, and she became the most accomplished pickpocket and thief in Cairo within a year.

When she was 12, Ororo felt a strong urge to head south and reconnect with her familial roots, and she journeyed alone across the Sahara Desert. Finally, she reached her ancestors' homeland: the Serengeti Plain. By adolescence, her mutant ability to manipulate the weather had emerged, and she used it to aid the local tribes, who worshipped her as the Storm Goddess.

Professor X convinced her to abandon the sheltered world she had surrounded herself with so that she could use her great powers to benefit the entire world. Hated and feared for her strange and frightening abilities—not revered, as she had been in Africa—Ororo has stood fast with the X-Men in their attempts to promote peaceful coexistence between man and mutant. Except for brief periods away from the team, she has remained a member ever since, even through the temporary loss of her mutant abilities.

While she commands Mother Nature's bountiful gifts, Ororo is capable of unleashing the catastrophic fury of the elements. One with the Earth, she truly understands the sanctity of life and feels a strong obligation to help preserve it in all its forms—man or mutant, plant or animal, good or evil.

Marvel Heroes

Thing

Intro

Once a skilled fighter-pilot, Ben Grimm is now the Thing, a member of the world-famous Fantastic Four. Bathed in cosmic radiation during a fateful trip with his three friends, Ben was transformed into a hideous creature of craggy, orange stone with superhuman strength.

Profile

Real Name:	**Benjamin Jacob Grimm**
Occupation:	**Adventurer**
Group Affiliation:	**Fantastic Four**
Base of Operations:	**New York**
Height:	**6'**
Weight:	**500 lbs.**
Eye Color:	**Blue**
Hair Color:	**Brown** (human form); **none** (Thing form)

Power Grid

Intelligence
Strength
Speed
Durability
Energy Projection
Fighting Skills

POWER SUMMARY

SUMMARY ITEM	DESCRIPTION
Strengths	Shockwave effect on many attacks,can block super far attacks
Weaknesses	No long-range attacks, too heavy to wall run, 2-hit combos only
Environmental Advantages	Resistant to acid and fire and receives minimal damage when smashing through objects
Environmental Disadvantages	Can't recover from ring-out situations, electricity causes damage and stuns
Combat Strategies	Object throws, character throws, super combo attacks
Defensive Strategies	Normal blocking, super blocking, redirecting, dodging

SPECIAL MOVES, JUGGLES, AND CRITICAL HITS

SPECIAL MOVES

Move Type	*Move Name*	*Xbox*	*PS2/PSP*	*NGC*
Super Attack 1	Ground Smash (shockwave)	X+R	■+R1	A+R
Super Attack 2	Hand Clap (shockwave)	X+R	■+R1	A+R
Super Far Attack	Ground Smash (shockwave)	X+R	■+R1	A+R
Super Throw	Crush Head Toss (shockwave)	B+R	●+R1	X+R
Super Jump Attack (ascending)	In-Air Hand Clap (shockwave)	A, X+R	×, ■+R1	B, A+R
Super Jump Attack (descending)	Single Fist Ground Slam (shockwave)	A, X+R	×, ■+R1	B, A+R
Super Attack Stomp	Elbow Drop (shockwave)	X+R	■+R1	A+R
Super Rising Attack	Ground Pound Standup (shockwave)	X+R	■+R1	A+R
Mobility Attack	Shoulder Ram	X	■	A
Mobility Super Attack	Jumping Ground Smash (shockwave)	X+R	■+R1	A+R
Dodge Super Attack	Ground Pound (shockwave)	D-pad+Y,X+R	D-pad+▲,■+R1	D-pad+Y,A+R
Super Air Tackle	Throw Down Crush (shockwave)	B+R	●+R1	X+R

CRITICAL HITS (HIGH-DAMAGE ATTACKS)

Attack Type	*Move Name*
Super Far Attack	Ground Smash
Super Throw	Crush Head Toss
Super Rising Attack	Ground Pound Standup
Super Dodge Attack	Ground Pound
Finishing Move	5x Slams

JUGGLING MOVES

Last Regular Attack	
Last Super Attack	
Mobility Regular Attack	•
Mobility Super Attack	
Rising Attack	•
Rising Super Attack	
Dodge Regular Attack	•
Dodge Super Attack	

Fighting-Against Strategies

Imagine being hit by a train, or having a mountain fall on your head—that may help you to understand the incalculable strength of the Thing. While he lacks technical fighting skills, he compensates for it with attacks so powerful they cause shockwaves strong enough to knock over nearby opponents. Here's a rundown of what you can expect to see from an AI-controlled Thing:

1. **Thrown Objects**
2. **Wielded Weapons**
3. **Body Throws**
4. **Regular Attacks**
5. **Super Attacks**

Here are some tips to help you along the way:

Tactics

- You can't overpower him, but you can outfight him. If your fighter has solid technical ability and speed, get in some super attack combinations and then get out of the way of Thing's brutal counterattack.
- Thing doesn't take to the air very often, and if he does it's for one of two reasons: he's going to cause a shockwave with his next attack or he's going after someone above him with an air tackle.
- If you're going to throw something at him, make it a super throw or you're wasting your time. Thing doesn't even have to block regularly thrown objects, they just bounce off him or are effortlessly redirected.
- Explosions work wonders; use the knockback effect of explosions to help push Thing toward potential ring outs.
- If you've got a ranged attack, use it. The farther Thing is away from you the better. Even his shockwaves have a maximum range—if you can stay outside this range you're golden. Now just keep dodging those flying cars.

History

Recruited by Reed Richards to pilot his experimental starship, Ben was opposed to Reed's idea for an unauthorized test flight, warning that the ship's shielding might prove inadequate protection against intense radiation. But he stood by his best friend, reluctantly consenting to take the pilot's seat. Rounding out the four-person crew were Reed's fiancée Sue Storm and her kid brother Johnny.

In space, Ben tried desperately to maintain control when the starship unexpectedly encountered intense radiation, but was forced to abort the flight. Surviving Ben's crash-landing in the New Jersey woods, all four discovered that the cosmic rays had mutagenically altered their bodies.

Ben's freakish transformation was perhaps the most shocking: He was horrified to find that he had become an orange-colored, thick-skinned, heavily muscled, superhumanly strong "thing"—and unlike his friends, he could not return to normal. Grudgingly, the morose Ben agreed to help his friends use their unique powers for humanity's benefit. Ben at first was angered by his condition but eventually became resigned to his fate, though he was no less miserable.

Ben is his own worst enemy: In his eyes, he is a monster—but as a member of the world-famous Fantastic Four, he is the idol of millions. Despite his outlook, the blue-eyed Thing has maintained his sense of humor and honor. Under his rocky, streetwise exterior, there beats an ever-lovin' heart of gold. But when clobberin' time comes around, the fiercely loyal Ben isn't afraid to use his brawn to back up his beloved teammates.

MARVEL HEROES

VENOM

INTRO

Utterly insane and totally without remorse, Venom is the antithesis of his adversary, Spider-Man. Driven entirely by a single base emotion, Venom comprehends only its all-consuming desire for revenge.

PROFILE

REAL NAME:	Eddie Brock
OCCUPATION:	Criminal
GROUP AFFILIATION:	None
BASE OF OPERATIONS:	Mobile
HEIGHT:	6' 3"
WEIGHT:	260 lbs.
EYE COLOR:	Blue
HAIR COLOR:	Reddish-blond

POWER GRID

Attribute	Rating (of 7)
INTELLIGENCE	2
STRENGTH	4
SPEED	2
DURABILITY	4
ENERGY PROJECTION	1
FIGHTING SKILLS	2

Power Summary

SUMMARY ITEM	DESCRIPTION
Strengths	Super strength, swinging, wall climbing, ranged web attacks, long-range throws
Weaknesses	Fire does extra damage
Environmental Advantages	Walls, can recover from ring-out situations
Environmental Disadvantages	Fire does extra damage
Combat Strategies	Swinging attacks, wall attacks, object throws
Defensive Strategies	Block, super block, redirecting, dodging

Tip

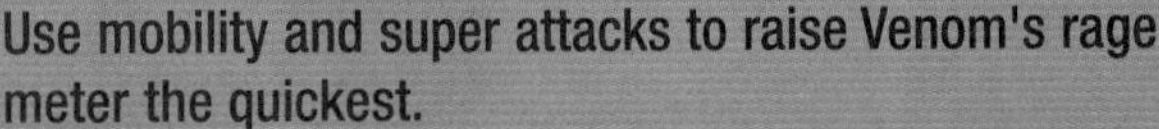

Use mobility and super attacks to raise Venom's rage meter the quickest.

Special Moves, Juggles, and Critical Hits

SPECIAL MOVES

Move Type	*Move Name*	*Xbox*	*PS2/PSP*	*NGC*
Mobility Move (air)	Web Swing	L	L1	L
Mobility Move (ground)	Zipline	L	L1	L
Mobility Move	Wall Climb	D-pad+L+R	D-pad+L1+R1	D-pad+L+R
Super Far Attack	Web Bullets	X+R	■+R1	A+R
Super Throw	Web Pull to Whiplash	B+R	●+R1	X+R

CRITICAL HITS (HIGH-DAMAGE ATTACKS)

Attack Type	*Move Name*
Super Attack 3 (3rd hit in combo)	Left-Hand Web Ground to Side Drop Kick
Super Dodge Attack	Web Bullets
Super Throw	Web Pull to Whiplash
Wall Hang Super Attack	Web Bullets
Super Rising Attack	Web Bullets
Mobility Attack	Corkscrew Kick (from jump, swing, or zipline)
Finishing Move	Bite'n'Toss

JUGGLING MOVES

Last Regular Attack	•
Last Super Attack	
Mobility Regular Attack	
Mobility Super Attack	
Rising Attack	•
Rising Super Attack	
Dodge Regular Attack	•
Dodge Super Attack	

Tip

Venom can grab props from a distance by pushing Super and Throw.

Tip

Venom can throw opponents from a distance by pushing Super and Throw. This is a super way to throw your opponent over the edge for a ring out.

Caution

Venom takes massive damage from fire—avoid it at all costs!

fighting-against strategies

Venom is all about wreaking havoc on his enemies in any way, shape, or form—he doesn't want to just beat you, he wants to destroy you. Be prepared for him to throw everything at you in a very erratic manner! Here are a few frequent elements you'll see when fighting an AI Venom:

1. Swinging Attacks
2. Ranged Attacks
3. Object Throws

Use these tactics to battle the rage and fury that is Venom:

tactics

- Venom is so tough and fast that he doesn't bother blocking, so he tends to take cumulative damage this way. He'll try to dodge most of what you throw at him instead. Use this to your advantage: throw objects at him, use ranged attacks, or get in close for super attacks and throws.
- He doesn't use many air tackles, so feel free to jump around him with near impunity. Use air attacks that come down on him hard from above.
- Venom won't try to throw you that often. Get in close and when his super attack combos miss their mark, move in for the kill with your own super combos and throws.
- If Venom is climbing a wall, get out of the way. His wall attacks are powerful and dangerous. If you have time, grab a barrel and knock him down with the impact and explosion.
- Venom is another character who can lift all Class 3 objects and hurl them at you—rest assured he'll be doing just that! If you can't catch or redirect large objects, make sure you're quick enough to find cover.
- As long as Venom has SP in his meter, he'll be slinging web bullets at you. His ranged attacks are powerful: if you can't find cover, get in close and take the fight to him!
- Venom only uses rising attacks half the time: if he's prone, lay the boots to him for the extra damage!
- When Venom's web-swinging, steer clear of his path. Give him a wide berth until he's back on solid ground.

caution

Always know where your best cover is when fighting Venom—his web bullets cause high damage that adds up fast.

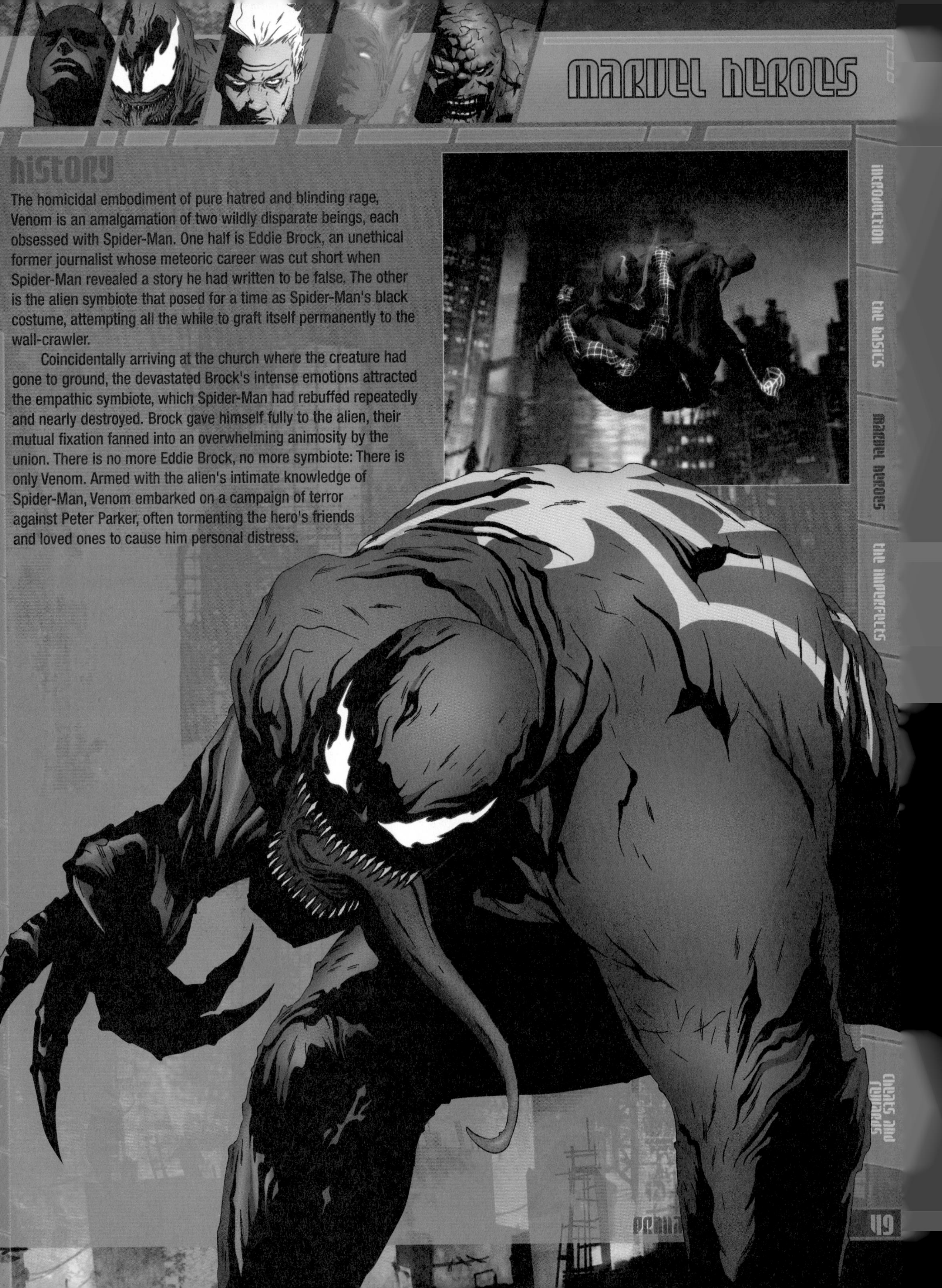

History

The homicidal embodiment of pure hatred and blinding rage, Venom is an amalgamation of two wildly disparate beings, each obsessed with Spider-Man. One half is Eddie Brock, an unethical former journalist whose meteoric career was cut short when Spider-Man revealed a story he had written to be false. The other is the alien symbiote that posed for a time as Spider-Man's black costume, attempting all the while to graft itself permanently to the wall-crawler.

Coincidentally arriving at the church where the creature had gone to ground, the devastated Brock's intense emotions attracted the empathic symbiote, which Spider-Man had rebuffed repeatedly and nearly destroyed. Brock gave himself fully to the alien, their mutual fixation fanned into an overwhelming animosity by the union. There is no more Eddie Brock, no more symbiote: There is only Venom. Armed with the alien's intimate knowledge of Spider-Man, Venom embarked on a campaign of terror against Peter Parker, often tormenting the hero's friends and loved ones to cause him personal distress.

Marvel Heroes

Wolverine

Intro

Little is known of his past, save that it was fraught with pain and loss. Long ago, he trained as a samurai in Japan; later, he became Weapon X, an operative for the Canadian government. Today, Logan is an X-Man—using his animal-keen senses, healing factor, and razor-sharp claws to help protect a world that fears and hates mutants.

Profile

Real Name:	Logan
Occupation:	Adventurer
Group Affiliation:	X-Men
Base of Operations:	New York
Height:	5' 3"
Weight:	195 lbs.
Eye Color:	Brown
Hair Color:	Black

Power Grid

Attribute	Rating (of 7)
Intelligence	2
Strength	4
Speed	2
Durability	4
Energy Projection	1
Fighting Skills	7

Tip: Mobility and super attacks work best to increase Logan's rage meter.

POWER SUMMARY

SUMMARY ITEM	DESCRIPTION
Strengths	Fast ground movement, wall running and climbing, health regenerates, many juggle attacks
Weaknesses	No long-range attacks
Environmental Advantages	Can aggressively use walls to his advantage
Environmental Disadvantages	Electricity causes damage, cannot recover from ring-out situations
Combat Strategies	Super combo attacks, wall attacks, dodging attacks
Defensive Strategies	Dodging, normal blocking, redirecting, super blocking

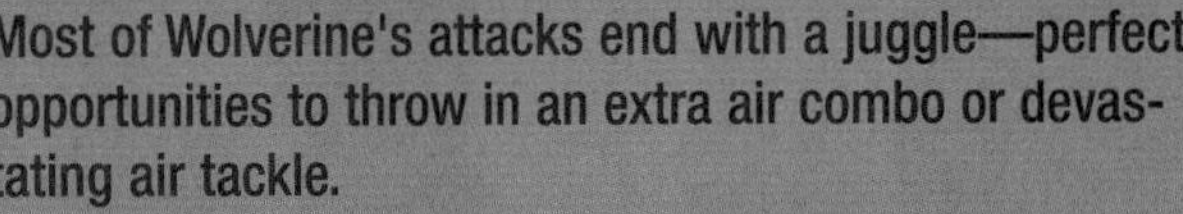

TIP

Most of Wolverine's attacks end with a juggle—perfect opportunities to throw in an extra air combo or devastating air tackle.

SPECIAL MOVES, JUGGLES, AND CRITICAL HITS

SPECIAL MOVES

Move Type	*Move Name*	*Xbox*	*PS2/PSP*	*NGC*
Mobility Move	Wall Run	D-pad+L	D-pad+L1	D-pad+L
Mobility Move	Wall Hang	D-pad+L+R	D-pad+L1+R1	D-pad+L+R
Super Throw	Claw Toss	B+R	●+R1	X+R

CRITICAL HITS (HIGH-DAMAGE ATTACKS)

Attack Type	*Move Name*
Super Attack 1	Left Slash
Super Attack 2	Gut Stab
Super Attack 3	Uppercut Claw Slash
Super Far Attack	Double Downward Claw Slash
Super Throw	Stab Throw
Super Jump Attack (ascending)	Twirl Slash
Super Jump Attack (descending)	Double Claw Dive
Wall Run Attack	Double Fist Dive
Super Wall Run Attack	Double Claw Dive
Super Wall Hang Attack	Double Claw Dive
Super Stomp Attack	Double Claw Stab
Super Rising Attack	Uppercut Slash
Super Mobility Attack	Single Claw Sliding Uppercut
Super Dodge Attack	Backhand Uppercut Slash
Super Air Tackle	Claw Stab Throw
Finishing Move	Multiple Claw Slashes

JUGGLING MOVES

Move	
Last Regular Attack	
Last Super Attack	•
Mobility Regular Attack	
Mobility Super Attack	•
Rising Attack	•
Rising Super Attack	•
Dodge Regular Attack	•
Dodge Super Attack	•

Fighting-Against Strategies

Think of a rabid wolverine having a bad day to sum up Logan's attitude and fighting style. He attacks from any angle, position, or situation—it's a type of organized chaos. With the most combination and juggle options, he's the worst threat up close. Logan is very unpredictable, but here are a the common trends you'll see when fighting his AI:

1. Jumping Attacks and Tackles
2. Super Attacks
3. Rising Attacks
4. Dodging Attacks
5. Juggles
6. Wall Running and Climbing Attacks
7. Mobility Attacks

And here are a few suggestions to help prevent him getting his claws on you, in you, or right through you:

Tactics

- Ranged attacks work best.
- Hit-and-run tactics work well, but keep the pressure on him so he can't regenerate the losses you're causing.
- When Logan is in rage mode, stay away from him at all costs! His rage lasts for 20 seconds, so use the time to grab something to throw at him and keep him at bay.
- From a prone position he commonly attacks with a vicious rising super attack: don't be standing around trying to foot stomp him or you're likely to get a face full of adamantium. Instead, this is a good time to hit him with explosive props and weapons.
- Don't jump around him too much; he's very good at grabbing hold and slamming you back down to ground level.
- Most of his attacks will be superpowered—let him expend his SP meter before going in close for the kill.
- Access to walls makes Logan really dangerous because his attacks launched from wall-running and climbing can do a lot of damage (especially his wall run super attack!). Keep an eye on how he's behaving around the arena walls before you decide to move in.
- Mobility Attacks: Logan is fast on the ground and can attack from a distance quite effectively. If he's running at you, get out of the way or hit him with a thrown prop.

Caution

Wolverine is the ultimate scrapper—don't try standing toe-to-toe with him to duke it out. You're only going to get hurt that way.

History

In the latter half of the 20th century, the Canadian government subjected Logan to a bizarre battery of experiments intended to forge the ultimate killing machine. Weapon X scientists grafted the indestructible metal adamantium to Logan's skeleton and bone claws, and introduced memory implants that shaped his past to suit their ends. Combined with the earlier effects of his healing factor, these false memories have made it impossible for Logan to discern fact from fiction when recalling his former life. He now knows little of his past, save that it was fraught with pain and loss.

Wolverine was working as an operative for the Canadian government when he accepted Professor X's offer to join the X-Men. Logan chose to stay on partly out of his belief in Xavier's vision for the co-existence of humans and mutants, and partly because of his attraction to Jean Grey.

During his time with the X-Men, Logan has worked to regain his lost memories, but virtually every answer leads him to even more new questions. Although he would rarely admit it, Logan remains with the X-Men because he feels the team is the closest thing he has to a family in the world. Serving with the X-Men has given Logan what he had been missing for so long: a cause worth fighting for.

Still somewhat uncontrollable and unpredictable in battle, and prone to an occasional berserker rage, Wolverine has proven to be a tremendous asset to the team; he continues to make his home in Xavier's mansion. Haunted by half-forgotten demons, he fights for those who can't fight for themselves.

the imperfects
brigade

intro

With the intelligence, strength, and density of 100 men, Brigade was a 21st century Frankenstein war machine. His big and ugly size was the brutal embodiment of the marine platoon he led in his past life. Now, haunted by a massive case of Dissociative Identity Disorder (DID), he struggles to cope with all the voices that relentlessly torment him.

profile

real name:	Sgt. Rick Landau
occupation:	Army Sergeant (among 100 others)
group affiliation:	"The Imperfects"
base of operations:	Fort Worth
height:	7' 6"
weight:	800 lbs.
eye color:	Black
hair color:	Black

power grid

intelligence
strength
speed
durability
energy projection
fighting skills

Power Summary

SUMMARY ITEM	DESCRIPTION
Strengths	Long-range attacks, super strength, resistant to all types of damage, quick SP regeneration
Weaknesses	Schizoid seizures (temporarily incapacitated during battles)
Environmental Advantages	Resistant to acid, fire, electricity
Environmental Disadvantages	Can't recover from ring-out situations
Combat Strategies	Super far attacks (cannons), object throws, super attack combos
Defensive Strategies	Normal blocks, super blocks, redirects, dodging

Special Moves, Juggles, and Critical Hits

SPECIAL MOVES

Move Type	*Move Name*	*Xbox*	*PS2/PSP*	*NGC*
Super Attack	Cannon Blast	X+R	■+R1	A+R
Super Far Attack	Cannon Blast	X+R	■+R1	A+R
Super Throw	Cannon Blast Throw	B+R	●+R1	X+R
Mobility Super Attack	Double Missile Fire	X+R	■+R1	A+R
Super Air Tackle	Throw Down, Cannon Blast	B+R	●+R1	X+R

CRITICAL HITS (HIGH-DAMAGE ATTACKS)

Attack Type	*Move Name*
Super Far Attack	Cannon Blast
Super Throw	Cannon Blast Throw
Super Rising Attack	Rising Cannon Blast
Super Dodge Attack	Cannon Blast
Finishing Move	All Weapons Blast

JUGGLING MOVES

Last Regular Attack	•
Last Super Attack	
Mobility Regular Attack	•
Mobility Super Attack	
Rising Attack	•
Rising Super Attack	
Dodge Regular Attack	•
Dodge Super Attack	

tip You can rapid fire Brigade's cannons by mashing the super attack buttons. But if you run out of superpower, he stuns himself and is vulnerable for a few seconds. If Brigade ever goes into Rage mode, watch out because he will rapid fire you to death.

fighting-against strategies

If it moves, blast it! Crush it! Kill it! That seems to be Brigade's prime directive. He's not a finesse fighter, but what he lacks in technical ability he makes up for in firepower! Here's what to expect when fighting an AI Brigade:

1. Ranged Attacks (Cannon Blast)
2. Mobility Attacks (shoulder rams and missiles)
3. Throws (both body and objects)
4. Melee Attacks (regular and super)

Don't get caught in his sights or he'll blow you away like a clown out of a cannon. Use these tips to help keep you safe:

tactics

- Brigade doesn't care about dodging attacks; in fact he doesn't feel pain much anymore, so he'll take whatever you throw at him. He blocks only half the time due to his inherent damage resistance. Use this to your advantage and just keep whittling him down one attack at a time.
- Be very cautious when attacking a prone Brigade; half the time he'll execute his super rising attack, which does critical damage.
- Brigade super blocks often because his recharge rate is so high. Take advantage of the period right after he super blocks and attack immediately while he's low on juice.
- Destroy as many of the arena's objects as you can—this reduces the amount of potential weapons Brigade has available to use against you.
- Mobile fighters should use a hit-and-run strategy using their best combinations, juggles, and air tackles. He's a big target and he's easy to grab hold of in the air.
- Watch carefully for his seizures to kick in—when he's distracted and temporarily incapacitated. It's time to strike hard and fast: hit him with some critical damage attacks and super combos!

HISTORY

During the invasion of Iraq, a U.S. Marine Recon platoon was gassed by Iraqi troops during an ambush—or so the public was told. In fact, a "black bag" operation, led by elements of the CIA, went awry and a nerve agent, planted to be connected to Iraqi forces, detonated prematurely. Coincidentally, Van Roekel's scientists were looking to explore areas of tissue-regeneration and multiple brain stem merging. They seized the opportunity and with the exchange of a significant amount of money, Van Roekel's team acquired the bodies. The corpses were perfect specimens: intact and filled with the lethal bio-weapon gas mixture, their flesh was still alive.

Elements of the 100-man platoon were combined to form a single soldier: tendons, muscular density, veins, arteries, and skin were fused into a nightmarish combination. With remolded and heavily armored alien cybernetic arms, brain matter (constructed of neural processors and cranial chemicals) the concoction was mixed and reformatted to support and follow a singular consciousness—the former platoon's commanding officer, Rick Landau.

But, it was a work in progress, and certain mental "irregularities" had not been perfected. Brigade was prone to fits of schizophrenic seizures where any number of his former teammates' personalities broke out, rejecting the singular identity. Now, his nightmares and bouts of depression are at times incapacitating. At night, in his bed, whispers of betrayal and the military's "training accident" torment his mind. Even a steady diet of high-level antidepressants is unable to quell the pain. Ironically Van Roekel's scientists are unsure how this "almost perfect" war machine will react to the stress of combat.

the imperfects

FAULT ZONE

intro

A true waif, Fault Zone can "tune" into the resonate frequency of her environment and cause seismic disturbances. With a seismic generator grafted to her arm and connected straight to her nervous system, Fault Zone can create vibrations that cause massive localized geological aftershocks.

profile

real name:	Maria Peterov
occupation:	Adventurer
group affiliation:	"The Imperfects"
base of operations:	Moscow
height:	5' 9"
weight:	95 lbs.
eye color:	Gray
hair color:	Black

power grid

- intelligence
- strength
- speed
- durability
- energy projection
- fighting skills

Power Summary

SUMMARY ITEM	DESCRIPTION
Strengths	Shockwave attacks, high mobility, wall running, wall hanging
Weaknesses	No long-range attacks
Environmental Advantages	Can aggressively use walls to her advantage
Environmental Disadvantages	Can't recover from ring-out situations
Combat Strategies	Super combo attacks, super jump attacks, shockwave techniques
Defensive Strategies	Dodging, normal blocking, super blocking, redirecting

tip

Use Fault Zone's super attacks to get her into Rage mode the fastest.

Special Moves, Juggles, and Critical Hits

SPECIAL MOVES

Move Type	*Move Name*	*Xbox*	*PS2/PSP*	*NGC*
Mobility Move	Wall Run	D-pad+L	D-pad+L1	D-pad+L
Mobility Move	Wall Hang	D-pad+L+R	D-pad+L1+R1	D-pad+L+R
Super Far Attack	Stab into Ground Shockwave	X+R	■+R1	A+R
Mobility Super Attack	Jumping Ground Attack	X+R	■+R1	A+R
Super Air Tackle	Shockwave Stick'n'Blast	B+R	●+R1	X+R

CRITICAL HITS (HIGH-DAMAGE ATTACKS)

Attack Type	*Move Name*
Super Attack 3	Double Sticks into Ground Shockwave
Super Far Attack	Stab into Ground Shockwave
Super Throw	Front Walk Over Shockwave
Wall Hang Super Attack	Corkscrew Dive
Super Rising Attack	Shockwave Getup
Dodge Super Attack	Stab Sticks into Ground Shockwave
Finishing Move	Shock Treatment

JUGGLING MOVES

Last Regular Attack	•
Last Super Attack	
Mobility Regular Attack	
Mobility Super Attack	
Rising Attack	•
Rising Super Attack	
Dodge Regular Attack	•
Dodge Super Attack	

Fighting-Against Strategies

As a former performer, Fault Zone literally dances circles around her opponents. Her high mobility and low physical strength make her perfect for hit-and-run attacks. Although she has the same shockwave attack effect as Thing, she's a whole new breed of opponent. Here are the most common elements when fighting against an AI Fault Zone:

1. **Super Combo Attacks (shockwaves)**
2. **Melee Combo Attacks**
3. **Jumping Attacks (shockwaves)**
4. **Super Mobility Attacks**

Use the following tactics to keep Fault Zone from turning you into her own private epicenter:

Tactics

- Fault Zone has no long-ranged attacks. This is the easiest advantage to use against her. Use long-range attacks or hurled weapons to quickly beat her down.
- She dodges attacks more than any other defensive tactic. If you're going to throw objects at her, use lighter ones that travel faster—don't give her time to move away.
- Her super rising attack is especially dangerous with its high damage and knockback effect. Better stay clear of her when she's down.
- Fault Zone has a long Rage mode, approximately 20 seconds. While she's charged up, she does tons of super combos—this is when she's most dangerous, as the shockwave gives her lots of time to set up the next combo while you're down. Keep her at a distance while she's raging!
- Some fighters have to take the scrap to her. In this situation, you must make your attacks most effective before a shockwave blasts you out of the park. Full combos with juggles and follow-up air attacks or air tackles are mandatory here!

history

Maria grew up in modern-day Moscow, and from a young age, demonstrated a natural gift for dancing. She became the youngest prodigy at the Imperial Russian Ballet where her skill, sensitivity, and discipline were far beyond that of most professionals. As a teenager she starred in several productions and became a world-renowned icon of dance.

At the tender age of 15, on the opening night of her lead role in Tchaikovsky's *Swan Lake* in Los Angeles, Maria was in a terrible car accident. An earthquake struck an elevated highway that collapsed, instantly killing her parents and leaving her a quadriplegic. She would never dance or walk again. Retreating into seclusion, she grew angry at the loss of her family and her stolen dreams. To her, life was a cruel joke. She hated the world.

Across the planet, Van Roekel was in search of a nimble and young test subject. He had created a seismic accelerator that would allow its possessor to create localized geological aftershocks, but the device required precise control to be able to master it. Only someone who had amazing muscle memory and control could use it. He had read about Maria and sent his recruiters to convince her to join his top-secret program.

Van Roekel offered to return Maria's ability to walk. He promised to replace her atrophied muscles and damaged nerves with cybernetics. It was an offer she could not refuse. At the same time Van Roekel attached his seismic weapon through her nervous system and taught her how to control its terrible power. Maria quickly mastered her newfound weapon. She enjoyed possessing a fantastic destructive power. It was a way she could get back at the world.

the imperfects
hazmat

intro

A brilliant scientist, Keith Kilham was responsible for creating immunization vaccines for the world's most dangerous substances…until he became a victim of his own success. A horrible lab accident left Kilham severely mutated, and his DNA destabilized. Van Roekel tamed the degenerative process, leaving Hazmat—a human toxic waste dump seeking revenge.

profile

real name:	Dr. Keith Kilham
occupation:	Researcher—Infectious Disease
group affiliation:	"The Imperfects"
base of operations:	Ohio
height:	7' 6"
weight:	210 lbs.
eye color:	White
hair color:	Unknown

power grid

intelligence	5
strength	3
speed	2
durability	4
energy projection	4
fighting skills	2

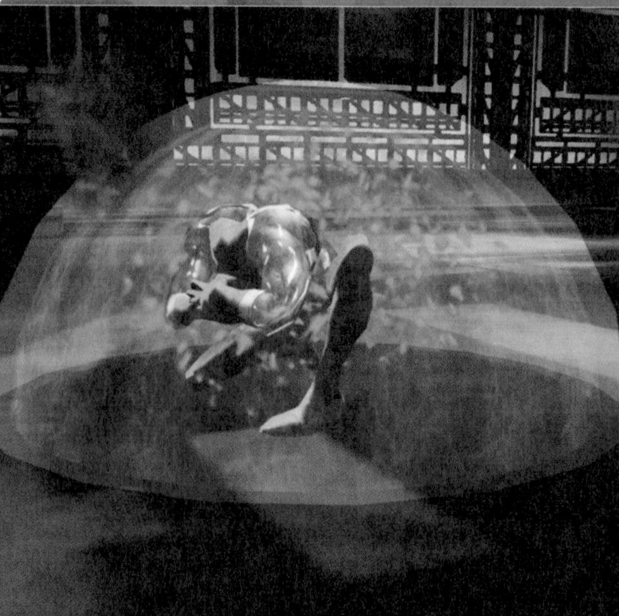

power summary

SUMMARY ITEM	DESCRIPTION
Strengths	Long-range attacks, swinging, wall climbing, zipline
Weaknesses	None
Environmental Advantages	Nearly immune to acid, can recover from ring-out situations, can make efficient use of arena walls
Environmental Disadvantages	None
Combat Strategies	Super far attacks, super combos, mobility attacks
Defensive Strategies	Normal blocking, dodging, super blocking, redirecting

special moves, juggles, and critical hits

SPECIAL MOVES

Move Type	*Move Name*	*Xbox*	*PS2/PSP*	*NGC*
Mobility Move	Swing	L	L1	L
Mobility Super Attack	Big Acid Blast	X+R	■+R1	A+R
Super Far Attack	Acid Blast	X+R	■+R1	A+R
Super Attack 3	Double Hand Ooze Flick	X+R	■+R1	A+R
Super Throw	Zipline (objects only)	B+R	●+R1	X+R
Super Throw	Vomit 'n' Toss (people only)	B+R	●+R1	X+R

CRITICAL HITS (HIGH-DAMAGE ATTACKS)

Attack Type	*Move Name*
Super Attack 3	Double Hand Ooze Flick
Super Attack Far	Acid Blast
Super Throw	Vomit 'n' Toss
Wall Run Super Attack	Acid Blast
Super Rising Attack	Acid Blast
Mobility Regular Attack 2 (while swinging)	Double Downward Claw Slash
Dodge Super Attack	Acid Blast
Finishing Move	Vomit Forcefeed

JUGGLING MOVES

Last Regular Attack	•
Last Super Attack	
Mobility Regular Attack	•
Mobility Super Attack	
Rising Attack	•
Rising Super Attack	
Dodge Regular Attack	•
Dodge Super Attack	

Fighting-Against Strategies

Hazmat has a very erratic fighting style that can be quite misleading. He's as mobile as Spider-Man, with long-range attacks, but he has some awkward rolling moves that make him more beastly and unpredictable. Here's what you can expect when fighting an AI Hazmat:

1. Super Far Attacks (Acid Blast)
2. Super Combo Attacks
3. Mobility Attacks (from swinging, wall running, wall climbing)
4. Air Attack Combos

Use our following techniques to help keep Hazmat's toxic vomit off your nice clean hero outfit:

Tactics

- Hazmat is quite mobile around any arena, but you'll still see a lot of ranged attacks (Acid Blasts) and Double Downward Claw Slashes while he's swinging.
- Jump attacks are another of his preferences, from which he is adept at executing both air attack combos and air tackles. Fight Hazmat on the ground for an advantage.
- Due to his potent long-range attacks, deal with him in close and personal with your arsenal of attack and super attack combos.
- Hazmat's Rage mode duration is approximately 10 seconds. If he gets there ahead of you, let him expend it while you take cover and then come back at him strong.
- He's good at both dodging and blocking incoming attacks—you may have to throw several nearby things at him to connect and do damage.

history

Doctor Keith Kilham was a quiet, unassuming, scientific nerd who worked for the U.S. Defense Science Board. He reported directly to the Pentagon and dealt with mankind's most lethal substances: the Ebola virus, anthrax, ricin, HCN, mustard gas, sarin gas, and VX gases. It was Dr. Kilham's job to find immunizations for the world's deadliest substances. Ironically, Kilham's own resistances were remarkably weak—he would catch every cold and flu around him and was endlessly popping meds so that he could continue working.

During a terrorist attack the lab was compromised during a tricky biological test. Safety containment procedures were rendered useless. Kilham had to react quickly. Several agents were on the verge of contaminating the main research facility, and the staff and the entire community were at risk. Despite the fact that his vaccines had yet to be tested on human subjects, Kilham injected himself with five highly unstable test immunity agents. He then rushed to the lab to secure the unleashed substances—hoping his vaccines would protect him.

The lab staff was quarantined for a month. Kilham told no one about the injections and was the only person to experience side effects from that fateful day. His body slowly started to dissolve as his molecular make-up shifted. He was becoming living mutation.

With help from his spies in the Pentagon, Van Roekel had Kilham kidnapped and brought to his secret research center. Van Roekel was fascinated by his unstable DNA. Was this the missing link that would allow humans to accept the alien grafts? Van Roekel devised a way to control Kilham's degenerative process and harness the power of his newfound molecular make-up. With a tech upgrade, the disfigured and severely mutated scientist was reborn as the terrifying Hazmat.

Driven by a desire to cure his state and find cures for all the chemical weapons that afflict humankind, Kilham ironically retains his mild-mannered nature and can be relied upon to deliver the most measured response to any crisis the Imperfects face. Even more ironically, he still pops pills to fight off colds.

the imperfects

johnny ohm

intro

An outlaw and criminal at heart, Johnny Ohm was also the toughest barroom brawler in South Carolina. His cries of innocence fell on deaf ears after a gruesome murder. Ohm was sentenced to death by electrocution but managed to survive it twice before a lightning storm delayed the execution. Johnny was later augmented to become a human lighting rod—a force to be reckoned with.

profile

real name:	John Ostrum
occupation:	Criminal and Psychopath
group affiliation:	"The Imperfects"
base of operations:	South Carolina
height:	6' 2"
weight:	190 lbs.
eye color:	Unknown
hair color:	Bald

power grid

intelligence	2
strength	3
speed	3
durability	3
energy projection	4
fighting skills	4

Power Summary

SUMMARY ITEM	DESCRIPTION
Strengths	Flying, long-range attacks
Weaknesses	None
Environmental Advantages	Nearly immune to electrical damage (in fact, electricity recharges his SP meter), can recover from ring-out situations
Environmental Disadvantages	None
Combat Strategies	Super far attacks (both air and ground), super combo attacks, object throws
Defensive Strategies	Normal blocking, dodging, redirecting, super block

tip

Use super attacks to raise Johnny's rage meter the fastest.

Special Moves, Juggles, and Critical Hits

SPECIAL MOVES

Move Type	*Move Name*	*Xbox*	*PS2/PSP*	*NGC*
Mobility Move	Fly	L	L1	L
Mobility Attack (while flying)	Air Ram	X	■	A
Super Far Attack	Lightning Bolt	X+R	■+R1	A+R
Super Throw	Lightning Blast	B+R	●+R1	X+R
Super Air Tackle	Lightning Back Blast	B+R	●+R1	X+R

CRITICAL HITS (HIGH-DAMAGE ATTACKS)

Attack Type	*Move Name*
Super Attack 1	1-Hand Palm Thrust
Super Attack 2	1-Hand Palm Thrust to Stomach
Super Attack 3	2-Hand Palm Thrust
Super Attack Far	Lightning Bolt
Super Throw	Lightning Blast Throw
Super Rising Attack	Rising Lightning Bolt
Dodge Super Attack	Lightning Blast
Finishing Move	Shock Therapy

JUGGLING MOVES

Last Regular Attack	•
Last Super Attack	
Mobility Regular Attack	
Mobility Super Attack	
Rising Attack	•
Rising Super Attack	
Dodge Regular Attack	•
Dodge Super Attack	

Fighting-Against Strategies

Johnny is a brawler, there are no fancy moves or high-agility techniques—he just wants to kick some serious butt any way he can, the dirtier the better. The no-nonsense street-fighting style combined with his electrical attacks make him a simple, straightforward menace. Here's what you can commonly expect from an AI Johnny Ohm:

1. **Super Far Attacks (air)**
2. **Super Far Attacks (ground)**
3. **Mobility Attacks (Air Ram)**
4. **Melee Attack Combos**
5. **Super Attack Combos**

Johnny is a living lightning rod. Here are some tactics to help keep him from giving you a serious case of static cling:

Tactics

- Johnny doesn't fly as much as he hovers, which helps him easily pull off air tackle after air tackle. If you're going up after him, be prepared, because he'll grab you and throw you down.
- Johnny is one of those rare fighters who's dangerous at both long and short range—the secret to beating him is being better at one or the other than he is. If you're a long-range fighter, beat him at that game. If you're a better melee fighter, beat him down in hand-to-hand combat.
- He won't super block often because he relies so heavily on his SP meter for ranged electrical attacks. Hurl everything you can get your hands on at him. He'll likely try to redirect most of it, but some will get through and knock him down—for more damage if he's knocked out of the air.

history

Johnny Ohm came of age in South Carolina in the 1950s. Johnny's family was so poor they could not even afford electricity. Bitter and ashamed of his lower-class roots, Johnny had an instant distrust for others. A true loner and rebel, he could barely contain his rage and was constantly on the lookout for trouble. He spent his life running afoul of the law—finally crossing the line from petty criminal to accused killer at the age of 24.

A particularly brutal barroom brawl ended with two black men dead and two police officers in the hospital. Johnny, found on the scene intoxicated and unconscious, was tossed into jail and quickly found guilty. Johnny stubbornly claimed his innocence but absolutely no one believed him. Johnny lost all hope and faith. The doctor relayed his opinion to the court—Johnny was labeled a threat to society with no remorse for his hideous crime. He was sentenced to death by electrocution.

Johnny's day of execution was a blip on the media's radar. But when the execution went awry, the media took a major interest. Johnny had taken the full brunt of the chair—twice—and survived. Just before the third attempt, lighting struck the facility and the power shortage stopped the execution in its tracks. Unconscious, with severe electrical burns across his body, Johnny was still alive. But before the authorities could reschedule his execution, the state legislature banned the death penalty. Johnny's sentence was commuted to life in prison and he was soon forgotten.

Decades later, one of the policemen involved in Johnny's case confessed to the murders on his deathbed. But nothing could bring back Johnny's will to live. Even legendary lawyer Matt Murdoch could not convince Johnny to fight for a new trial. At this point, Van Roekel's recruiters took an interest.

The prison released a statement to the press—Johnny Ohm had hung himself in his cell. In reality, Van Roekel's agents had arranged delivery of Ohm to the alien facility. Focusing on Ohm's high tolerance for extreme electrical current, the scientists explored ways for the charge to be used offensively. With Ohm's penchant for violence and emotional neutrality, he adapted easily to combat and strategy training. The man had found his natural calling—electric warrior. Will Johnny ever be able to convince himself of his own innocence and clear himself of this terrible crime?

the imperfects
PARAGON

intro

Cryogenically frozen for centuries, Paragon began life as a primitive soul named Maya. Uncluttered by the baggage of modern society and its politically correct morality, Maya's life was simple—to survive by any means necessary. Now, augmented with sophisticated alien technology, she has been groomed into the ultimate warrior. With savage human blood and enormous power, Paragon has unstoppable abilities.

profile

real name:	Maya
occupation:	Amazonian Warrior
group affiliation:	None
base of operations:	Amazon
height:	6' 0"
weight:	140 lbs.
eye color:	Blue
hair color:	Black

power grid

intelligence	3 of 7
strength	5 of 7
speed	4 of 7
durability	6 of 7
energy projection	3 of 7
fighting skills	6 of 7

Power Summary

SUMMARY ITEM	DESCRIPTION
Strengths	Long-range attacks (crystal shockwave attacks), bladed arms, teleporter, super strength
Weaknesses	None
Environmental Advantages	Can recover from ring-out situations, small arenas (i.e., Avengers' Mansion)
Environmental Disadvantages	None
Combat Strategies	Super far attacks, super mobility attacks, super combo attacks
Defensive Strategies	Redirecting, dodging, normal blocking, super blocking

Tip: Paragon's Super Throw will give her a small portion of health back.

Special Moves, Juggles, and Critical Hits

SPECIAL MOVES

Move Type	*Move Name*	*Xbox*	*PS2/PSP*	*NGC*
Mobility Move	Teleport	L	L1	L
Super Attack Far	Crystal Wave Attack	X+R	■+R1	A+R
Super Throw	Life Force Impale	B+R	●+R1	X+R
Super Air Tackle	Blade Stab Throw	B+R	●+R1	X+R
Finishing Move	Blade Impale	B+R	●+R1	X+R

CRITICAL HITS (HIGH-DAMAGE ATTACKS)

Attack Type	*Move Name*
Super Attack 3	Claw Attack
Super Attack Far	Crystal Wave Attack
Super Throw	Life Force Impale
Super Jump Attack (ascending)	Spinning Claw Slash
Super Jump Attack (descending)	Diving Claw Strike
Super Attack Stomp	Crystal Wave Attack
Super Rising Attack	Crystal Wave Attack
Dodge Super Attack	Crystal Wave Attack
Finishing Move	Blade Impale

JUGGLING MOVES

Last Regular Attack	•
Last Super Attack	
Mobility Regular Attack	
Mobility Super Attack	
Rising Attack	•
Rising Super Attack	
Dodge Regular Attack	•
Dodge Super Attack	

Note

Like The Wink, Paragon is also totally invincible during any of her teleportation moves.

Tip: Use any of Paragon's super attacks to quickly boost her rage meter.

Fighting-Against Strategies

Imagine for a moment, the results if you could create a fighter with retractable claws like Wolverine, teleportation like Nightcrawler, shockwave attacks like Thing, and energy-projection abilities like those of Storm or Magneto—meet Paragon! She is the perfect warrior; it's no wonder Van Roekel thinks of her as his crowning achievement! You don't have to wonder much about what her fighting style is like when you know whose abilities hers most resemble. However, let's break down the common elements in the fighting style of AI Paragon:

1. **Air Tackles**
2. **Throws (You! Not objects!)**
3. **Melee Attack Combos (regular and super)**
4. **Mobility Attacks (while teleporting)**
5. **Ranged Attacks (all variations of her Crystal Wave Attacks)**

There are no easy ways to defeat Paragon, but the following tactics will help in your battles:

Tactics

- Paragon's fighting skills, durability, and strength are incredibly high. Combined with her energy-projection abilities, there are few chinks in her armor. She has most aspects of combat covered, and you can't be a better all-round fighter than she is. However, what works best is to beat her at *one* thing: ranged attacks or in-close, hand-to-hand fighting. Choose based on your character's abilities: obviously Wolverine would fight in close, while Storm would focus on ranged lightning attacks.
- She will attempt to redirect most incoming object attacks rather than dodging them. Try throwing something at her and while she is distracted and redirecting it, follow up immediately with your mobility attacks to cover ground quickly.
- In close you need to watch her spinning blade attacks. They're very fast and it only takes that one move to knock you off your feet. Keep the pressure on her with all of your juggling attacks.

history

After a century-long search, a young, female Amazonian warrior, Maya, was chosen from an isolated, primitive, and forgotten society deep within the South American jungle. Matching a specifically required DNA structure, Maya was the perfect candidate for the ultimate weapon. Maya possessed a toxin-free physical make-up, Amazonian warrior skills, and the instinctual savagery found at the core of all humanity.

Having acquired the perfect specimen, Van Roekel ordered her to be put into a prolonged stasis. It would take years to successfully master the fusion of alien tech with humans before Van Roekel's team would finally be ready to work on Maya.

After "The Imperfects" were completed, project Paragon was set in motion. Working in a secret facility, the aliens downloaded tactics and combat information into Maya's brain. Her body was injected with chemicals to augment her already superior muscles and heighten her finely tuned senses. Training started shortly after—the girl was forced to fight and defend in various combat scenarios. Exercises were crafted to capitalize on and increase her natural ruthless brutality. It was always strike first and never ask questions.

When her mind and body were at peak performance, the alien symbiote was grafted to her spine. The painful transformation intertwined and fused her nerves and muscles with Van Roekel's own race. It was a tremendous success, as Paragon exceeded all of Van Roekel's expectations. She had become the ultimate killing machine.

But as Maya's awareness increased, so did her desire to escape her creator. The secret laboratory was nothing more than a prison and a threat to her future. During a particularly intense neural reprogramming session, Paragon seized the chance to surprise her captors and violently blaze her way out of the facility. No one would control her life again.

the imperfects
SOLARA

intro

As a baby, Reiko Kurokaki escaped unscathed from the fire that killed her mother. Recruited by Van Roekel's scientists, she became another step in his search to build the perfect warrior. He lined her body with alien crystals that burn at 2,000 degrees Celsius. As a result, Solara can incinerate any object known to mankind.

profile

real name:	Reiko Kurokaki
occupation:	Published scientist
group affiliation:	"The Imperfects"
base of operations:	Boston
height:	5' 8"
weight:	120 lbs.
eye color:	Yellow
hair color:	Bald

power grid

- intelligence
- strength
- speed
- durability
- energy projection
- fighting skills

INTRODUCTION
THE BASICS
MARVEL HEROES
THE IMPERFECTS
STORY MODE
ARENAS
ONLINE PLAY
CHEATS AND REWARDS

POWER SUMMARY

SUMMARY ITEM	DESCRIPTION
Strengths	Flying, long-range attacks, technical fighter (can execute four-hit combos)
Weaknesses	None
Environmental Advantages	Resistant to fire damage, can recover from ring-out situations
Environmental Disadvantages	None
Combat Strategies	Super far attacks (air), super far attacks (ground), super combo attacks
Defensive Strategies	Dodging, super block, normal block, redirecting

TIP

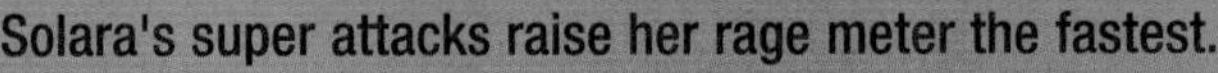

Solara's super attacks raise her rage meter the fastest.

SPECIAL MOVES, JUGGLES, AND CRITICAL HITS

SPECIAL MOVES

Move Type	*Move Name*	*Xbox*	*PS2/PSP*	*NGC*
Mobility Move	Fly	L	L1	L
Mobility Attack (flying)	Double-Fisted Air Ram	X	■	A
Super Far Attack (ground)	Flame Wall	X+R	■+R1	A+R
Super Throw (ground)	Heat Distortion Wave Throw	B+R	●+R1	X+R
Mobility Super Attack (flying)	Heat Distortion Wave	X+R	■+R1	A+R
Super Air Tackle (during flight or jump)	Heat Distortion Wave Air Tackle	B+R	●+R1	X+R

CRITICAL HITS (HIGH-DAMAGE ATTACKS)

Attack Type	*Move Name*
Super Attack 3	2-Hand Palm Thrust
Super Attack 4	Heat Distortion Wave
Super Attack Far	Flame Wall
Super Throw	Heat Distortion Wave Throw
Super Rising Attack	Flame Wall
Super Dodge Attack	Flame Wall
Finishing Move	Kiss of Death

JUGGLING MOVES

Last Regular Attack	
Last Super Attack	
Mobility Regular Attack	
Mobility Super Attack	
Rising Attack	•
Rising Super Attack	
Dodge Regular Attack	•
Dodge Super Attack	

TIP

Solara's resistance to fire is high. If her own attack gets reflected back to her, she will take little damage from it.

NOTE

In Solara's Super Attack 4, she touches the ground instead of the victim for the last two attacks.

Fighting-Against Strategies

Solara is highly mobile, with strong ranged attacks and solid technical fighting ability. She's one of the few characters who can execute four-hit combos. She is the Imperfects' "Torch" but her ranged attacks affect a wider swath. Below are the most common elements you see when battling an AI Solara:

1. **Super Far Attacks (air and ground: Flame Walls)**
2. **Mobility Attacks (Air Rams)**
3. **Super Mobility Attacks (Heat Distortion Waves)**
4. **Super Attacks (dodging, Rising Flame Walls)**
5. **Melee Combo Attacks (four-hit combos)**

Solara wants to make you a star; a bright, blazing body in the night. Use these tactics to keep things from getting too hot to handle:

Tactics

- Solara will send many Flame Walls your way, so keep moving. Due to the larger area of affect, they can even catch you while you're moving away. Be quick; let her focus and fire and then move out of the way and counterattack.
- Take her mobility advantages away from her. Let her come to you by finding and using cover in the arenas. Once on the ground she's much easier to deal with.
- Remember she's resistant to fire damage, so if you're playing a fire-based character, it's more effective to use physical attacks against her (objects and melee attacks).
- Her favored defensive maneuver is dodging; it usually works well for her given her high mobility. She also super blocks but only if she's got a lot of SP in reserve because she relies so much on her ranged attacks. If you catch her using super block often, come in and throw everything at her while she can't use her super combos and flame attacks.

history

In the middle of a ruthless gang war that had kept him underground and away from his wife for a year, the infamous Yakuza leader Kazuya Morimoto discovered that his wife had given birth to a daughter named Reiko. When he discovered that the child was actually fathered by one of his Yakuza rivals, Morimoto went insane with rage. While his wife and the infant Reiko slept, Morimoto poured gasoline in every room and burned the house to the ground. As he drove off, the distant screams of his wife cut through the winter night, but he did not stop.

When the maid returned in the morning, the house has been reduced to smoldering embers. She found baby Reiko miraculously in the middle of the burnt structure without a scratch. Reiko was kept a secret and sent to Cambridge to live with the maid's sister. There she grew up with a new identity and had no idea of her true past. Living a life of seclusion, Reiko was home schooled by her newfound family and showed an aptitude for quantum physics.

Years later she wrote her doctorate on sub-zero combustion. Her writings were *de facto* standard used by research facilities worldwide. After the theory was taken to scientific trials, Reiko was on the verge of a breakthrough. Instead, a terrible accident destroyed her university laboratory, killing dozens of workers and observers—including her adoptive parents—but once again, Reiko miraculously survived. Was the accident caused by sabotage from her father's agents?

Disgraced and having lost everything, she falls through the cracks, living in a slum and working under an assumed name as a cleaning woman at a community college physics lab, trying in vain to figure out what went wrong and complete her research. Niles Van Roekel identified Reiko and considered her a prime candidate. She was the daughter of a warrior, well versed in physics and particles, and had a mythical resistance to fire. Van Roekel gave her the clue to her failed experiment to recruit her and promised to restore her reputation in the scientific community.

Without a second thought, Reiko agreed to join his top-secret project. Van Roekel lined her insides with alien crystal and turned her into a human kiln. Now, her body can store high concentrations of energy and release it at targets. Whatever substance is in her vengeful wake is instantly incinerated.

The Imperfects

The Wink

Intro

The Wink, the daughter of Italy's most famous magician, was horribly disfigured because of her father's gambling debts, and she escaped death by mysteriously disappearing. Now, with a particle reactor implanted inside her, she can control every molecule inside her body. With it she can transpose dimensions and teleport short distances. Nothing would be a simple trick any more.

Profile

Real Name:	Benedetta Gaetani
Occupation:	Magician's assistant
Group Affiliation:	"The Imperfects"
Base of Operations:	Italy
Height:	5' 11"
Weight:	110 lbs.
Eye Color:	Yellow
Hair Color:	Unknown

Power Grid

Intelligence	3
Strength	2
Speed	4
Durability	2
Energy Projection	1
Fighting Skills	5

Power Summary

SUMMARY ITEM	DESCRIPTION
Strengths	Very fast movement, teleporting, gauntlet blades
Weaknesses	No long-range attacks, can't block super far attacks
Environmental Advantages	Can recover from ring-out situations
Environmental Disadvantages	Acid causes damage, electricity causes damage and stun
Combat Strategies	Mobility attacks, super combo attacks, body throws
Defensive Strategies	Dodging, redirecting, super blocking, normal blocking

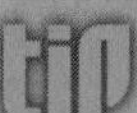

Tip

The Wink's Rage mode lasts approximately 20 seconds. Get her there fastest by using her super attacks.

Special Moves, Juggles, and Critical Hits

SPECIAL MOVES

Move Type	*Move Name*	*Xbox*	*PS2/PSP*	*NGC*
Mobility Move	Teleport	L	L1	L
Mobility Super Attack (during teleport)	Smokey 360 Whirlwind Attack	X+R	■+R1	A+R
Super Far Attack	Teleport Stomach Stab	X+R	■+R1	A+R
Super Throw (ground)	Teleport Throw	B+R	●+R1	X+R
Super Air Tackle (air)	Teleport Tackle to Ground	B+R	●+R1	X+R

CRITICAL HITS (HIGH-DAMAGE ATTACKS)

Attack Type	*Move Name*
Super Attack 1	Teleporting Rising Spin Attack
Super Attack 2	Teleport Stomach Stab
Super Attack 3	Teleport Whirlwind Slash
Super Attack Far	Teleport Stomach Stab
Super Throw	Teleport Throw
Super Rising Attack	Teleport Twirling Claw Slash
Dodge Super Attack	Smokey 360 Whirlwind Dive Attack
Finishing Move	Teleport Impale

JUGGLING MOVES

Last Regular Attack	•
Last Super Attack	
Mobility Regular Attack	
Mobility Super Attack	
Rising Attack	•
Rising Super Attack	
Dodge Regular Attack	•
Dodge Super Attack	

Fighting-Against Strategies

The Wink is quite similar in both abilities and fighting style to Paragon—armor, bladed gauntlets, teleportation. She's something of a prototype with her own flavor. The Wink makes extensive use of her teleportation abilities in most of her attacks. Here are the most common elements to her fighting style:

1. Mobility Attacks (via teleporting)
2. Melee Combo Attacks (both regular and super)
3. Air Tackles
4. Body Throws
5. Jump Attacks

Now you see her, now you don't. Here are some tactics to help keep The Wink in check:

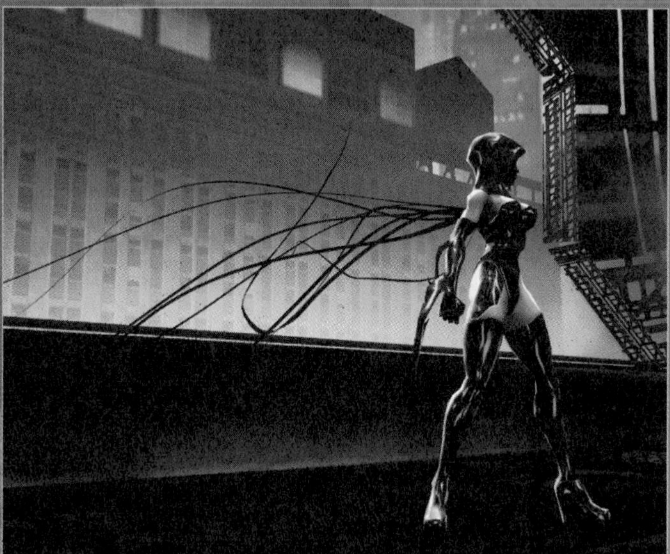

Tactics

- Even if she's not attacking immediately afterward, The Wink likes to keep her opponents guessing by teleporting to random locations. You can't hit her if you're constantly checking over your shoulder to find out where she is. When this happens frequently, back up and reassess the situation. Move far enough away to keep her in sight and pin her down with ranged attacks to prevent her from teleporting.
- If you're fighting The Wink in hand-to-hand combat and she's knocked down—back off! Her super rising attack does critical damage!
- In close-quarters combat, the third attack of her super melee combo is another one to watch out for—it also does critical damage.
- If you're a character with strong ranged attacks, we highly recommend using them. It makes battling The Wink so much easier when you can just line her up in your sights and take her out!

Note

The Wink is completely invincible when she teleports. You can't throw her if she is attacking, dodging, or doing anything that uses her teleporting ability. Depending on the game difficulty setting, she may also resist and break out of some or even most of your throw attempts.

history

Benedetta grew up the daughter of young Italian magicians—Aldo and Corazon Gaetani (The Great Gaetani). They took the magic world by storm, but the act was as much about Corazon's beauty as Aldo's deft touch. Benedetta suffered from the attentions of her mother, who was intensely disappointed with her shy, homely daughter. When Corazon mysteriously disappeared, Benedetta had grown into a beautiful young woman, maybe more beautiful than her departed mother.

As a recent widower, Aldo started to drink and gamble compulsively. He took his young daughter on tour throughout Italy as his new assistant. He became known as a superlative illusionist and started to tour the world because of his most famous trick—"The Disappearance." The trick made Benedetta, in plain view, disappear on stage and appear in a seat in the middle of the audience. Touted as the best illusionist that ever lived, Aldo stumped the experts. Some even said he was a mystic and his tricks were really miracles. Aldo started to believe that his tricks were real. Was Benedetta able to do this on her own?

He owed a lot of money to the wrong people. Blinded by his own fame, Aldo shrugged off the threats when he couldn't pay. But one night, when thugs again couldn't collect the money, they poured acid on his daughter's beautiful face. Benedetta was horribly disfigured. The thugs assassinated Aldo in his dressing room and then decided to finish off the only living witness—Benedetta. Benedetta performed her last act and vanished into thin air.

Strange rumors circulated about Aldo's murder and his daughter's disappearance, and Van Roekel and his scientists took notice. Van Roekel caught up with her in Spain. She needed someone to protect her and Van Roekel promised her complete safety. She had a particle reactor fused inside her left thigh that allowed her to control every molecule in her body. Now, using the fifth dimension she can phase and teleport short distances. No one would ever catch her again. The Wink was born.

The Imperfects

Niles Van Roekel

Intro

Desperate to save his home planet, Niles Van Roekel (a.k.a. Minuteman) grafted human beings with alien inventions. Six human experiments later, his crowning achievement, Paragon, was born. She would be mass produced and sent back to reclaim his home world from its oppressors.

Profile

Real Name:	Unknown dialect
Occupation:	Scientist/Inventor
Group Affiliation:	Alien race
Base of Operations:	Secret lab underground in New York City
Height:	6' 2"
Weight:	210 lbs.
Eye Color:	Blue
Hair Color:	Bald

Power Grid Van Roekel

- Intelligence
- Strength
- Speed
- Durability
- Energy Projection
- Fighting Skills

Power Grid Minuteman

- Intelligence
- Strength
- Speed
- Durability
- Energy Projection
- Fighting Skills

Power Summary

SUMMARY ITEM	DESCRIPTION (Minuteman Armor)
Strengths	Flight, long-ranged attacks, super strength, and protection from most types of damage
Weaknesses	High energy consumption (super attacks)
Environmental Advantages	Can recover from ring-out situations
Environmental Disadvantages	None
Combat Strategies	Super far attacks (air and ground), mobility attacks, and super combo attacks
Defensive Strategies	Normal blocking, redirecting, super blocking, dodging

Special Moves, Juggles, and Critical Hits

SPECIAL MOVES

Move Type	*Move Name*	*Xbox*	*PS2/PSP*	*NGC*
Mobility Move	Fly	L	L1	L
Mobility Attack (while flying)	Shoulder Air Ram	X	■	A
Super Far Attack (ground)	Energy Cannon Blast	X+R	■+R1	A+R
Super Mobility Attack (while flying)	2-Handed Energy Cannon Blast	X+R	■+R1	A+R
Super Air Tackle	Cannon Ground Blast	B+R	●+R1	X+R

CRITICAL HITS (HIGH-DAMAGE ATTACKS)

Attack Type	*Move Name*
Super Attack Far	Cannon Blast
Super Throw	Cannon Blast Throw
Super Jump Attack	Cannon Blast
Super Attack Stomp	Cannon Ground Blast
Super Rising Attack	Rising Cannon Blast
Mobility Super Attack	2-Handed Energy Cannon Blast
Super Dodge Attack	Cannon Blast
Finishing Move	Gutbuster to Guns Off

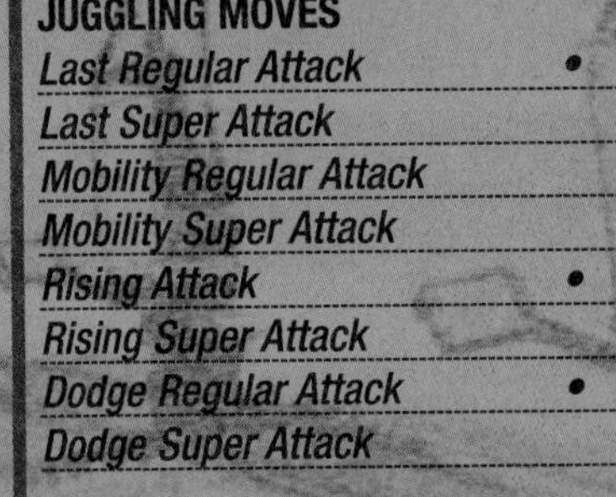

JUGGLING MOVES

Last Regular Attack	•
Last Super Attack	
Mobility Regular Attack	
Mobility Super Attack	
Rising Attack	•
Rising Super Attack	
Dodge Regular Attack	•
Dodge Super Attack	

introduction
the basics
marvel heroes
the imperfects
story mode
arenas
online play
cheats and rewards

fighting-against strategies

Van Roekel made the Minuteman suit to turn himself into a vicious killer—and it works! Aside from the predatory improvements made by his artificial nervous system, the suit is a fully functional weapons system. Here we list the AI Van Roekel's more common attacks:

1. **Ranged Attacks (Cannon Blasts)**
2. **Mobility Attacks (Air Rams and 2-Hand Cannons)**
3. **Super Air Tackles**
4. **Super Throws**

Use the following tactics to help defend Earth against Van Roekel and beat him down into the dirt!

tactics

- The Minuteman armor is very impressive, but with all its power Van Roekel is still limited in his melee fighting skills—he can only execute two-hit combos. Use this to your advantage by pushing him hard in close-quarters fighting.
- Van Roekel is dangerous in the air. He'll grab anything around him and blast it back down to ground level. His air tackles are very effective, so if you like flying or jumping attacks, stay outside his reach.
- On the ground Van Roekel is just as good with his body throws. If you're going in to fight him hand to hand, be aware of this. Use many dodging attacks to keep him from getting his hands on you.
- He'll throw every type of mobility and super attack at you, including many jumping attacks from which he fires his cannon blast. You must counter with much of your own blocking—this is truly one opponent where super blocking skills come in very useful.

history

Before his escape to Earth, Niles Van Roekel was a top-level scientist in his alien world. A highly respected academic and a patriot, Van Roekel proudly served his people. He was a leading authority in DNA research, sociology, biology, and art—the Leonardo da Vinci of his race. With his home world under oppression from occupying forces, Van Roekel and a contingent of military and scientific support staff fled their world with one objective in mind—to return with a weapon/army capable of overthrowing the enemy. No matter what it would take, what personal sacrifices would be required, Van Roekel was dedicated to the cause.

Over the last few decades, Van Roekel undertook monumental steps to acquire a facility, the necessary equipment, and test subjects needed to start the creation process. With a secret lab deep below the streets of New York (right under the humans' noses) Van Roekel began recruiting—usually by abducting—his test subjects. Van Roekel's first works failed, as frightening genetic mutations often led to the host's horrific death.

When a new plan was implemented, Solara, Johnny Ohm, Hazmat, Brigade, Fault Zone, and The Wink were all recruited. They were considered imperfect works in progress but still deemed highly successful in the long-term scheme. Finally, the warrior Paragon was developed. She was successfully fused with the alien symbiote, creating the ultimate weapon. Now all that was required was for Paragon to be mass-produced into an army that would liberate his home world.

For the grand return home, Van Roekel built the Minuteman suit of armor. His alien race's genetic makeup denied him the instinct and talent for aggression and war—but the Minuteman suit provided Van Roekel with an artificial nervous system based on his experiments with violent human subjects. Now Van Roekel himself could become a true warrior—and woe to any Imperfects who challenged his authority. It was a chance for him to look and feel like the victor and warrior he always wanted to be. The only thing that could ever get in Van Roekel's way was his own ego.

Story Mode

Introduction

The attack is already well underway. Much of New York has been devastated by alien invaders that seemed to come out of nowhere. Heroes are dead and many more are missing; the remaining members of various groups across the state have communicated to each other the need to work together. It's up to you to make sense of the chaos in the center of it all: New York City.

You will be faced with the sacrifice of many heroes throughout Story mode—those decisions are entirely up to you. Included in each character's section is the summary of his or her sacrifice mission, should you choose to give that hero up for the greater good. Choose wisely.

This section is divided by character; the order in which you play their missions is largely up to you once they have been unlocked. Keep in mind that you can have only four characters in your party before one must be sacrificed. You can play 100 percent of the game and complete all missions, or you may opt for the quickest route through Story mode; the latter is outlined in this chapter. The following list identifies the fastest mission completion path, but you won't be able to play the bonus missions nor unlock comics and some cards.

1. Thing 1
2. Wolverine 1–3
3. Elektra 1–3
4. Thing Sacrifice
5. Daredevil 1–3
6. Paragon 1
7. Storm 1–3
8. Daredevil Sacrifice
9. Venom 1–3
10. Paragon 2
11. Elektra Sacrifice
12. Spider-Man 1–3
13. Wolverine Sacrifice
14. Human Torch 1–3
15. Spider-Man Sacrifice
16. Iron Man 1–3
17. Iron Man Sacrifice
18. Magneto 1–3
19. Magneto Sacrifice
20. Paragon 3
21. Paragon 4

Van Roekel's Military Units

Ground Units

Invader

Invaders are gruesome fighting creatures built from human remains fused with alien technology. Though they retain high intelligence, their will is completely under the sway of their alien overlord. Almost completely immune to pain, these creatures can sustain heavy fire from conventional weapons. Their super-human strength and titanium alloy blades allow them to defeat virtually any opponent in close combat.

Decapitator

With genetic manipulation and advanced molecular-level surgery, Van Roekel has created these brutish creatures to act as shock-troops in his security forces. Decapitators are more advanced models compared to his original designs, the Invaders. Decapitators' size and strength have been boosted to levels that match the strength of the greatest superheroes on Earth.

The artificially dense bodies of Decapitators can withstand incredible amounts of punishment and they are armed with two alien-monofilament blades that can cut through virtually any material.

Eviscerator

To deal with armored targets, Van Roekel created these zombie-like mindless humanoids. They rapidly close in and grab their opponents with their powerful hooks. Then they activate anti-matter detonators that are embedded in their bodies. Their victim's only hope is to escape the deadly embrace before it is too late.

Mauler

As part of his experiment to arm the Imperfect called Fault Zone, Van Roekel invented the seismic claws that cause localized earthquakes. He equipped the Maulers with an early prototype version of these claws, which are less potent than those used by Fault Zone but deadly nonetheless. Van Roekel uses Maulers for digging the underground tunnels of his lair and blasting through bulkheads, as well as for wiping out human armored vehicles and troop formations.

Obliterator

Obliterators are mindless, living weapons armed with immense pulse cannons. Van Roekel created these grotesque creatures by melding human flesh with Turlin technology in order to provide his forces with much-needed long-range attack power.

The artificially enlarged body and heavy armor make the Obliterators walking tanks that can blast anything in their way. Their pulse cannons are more powerful than any human projectile weapon, strong enough to punch through even Iron Man's legendary armor.

Ravager

Lighter and more nimble, the Ravager is a modified design of Invader equipped with a light pulse cannon. Though they posses less firepower than the mighty Obliterators, Ravagers are nonetheless dangerous. Their weakness is their lack of body armor and the long time it takes for them to recharge their weapon.

Air Units

Marauder

Marauders are the vanguard of the alien invasion force, deadly flying machines armed with rapid-firing energy weapons. Inside their metal shell lies an antimatter reactor fused with a living human brain. The guiding brain has been reprogrammed to search and kill anything that lives.

Marauders are quick and nimble, able to hunt down and destroy even the fastest targets, such as human fighter jets—or even superheroes with the ability to fly!

Desolator

Designed to cause panic and to disperse enemy infantry formations, the Desolators have been developed from basic Desolator chassis. They drop anti-matter chargers that can cling to any known surface and will explode after a brief period of time. No known substance can withstand a direct hit from a Desolator explosive.

During Roekel's assault on New York, Desolator attacks forced almost the entire population of the great metropolis to evacuate.

Predator

Predator is a masterpiece of Turlin technology. With its advanced neural-enhanced brain and heat-seeking plasma missiles, Predator is the most advanced model of flying war machine mass-produced by Van Roekel. Brain implants that are used to guide the Predators were hand-picked by Van Roekel for their reflexes and excellent 3-D coordination.

Thing

The Invasion

Location: Brooklyn Bridge

Opponents: Invaders, Decapitator (Boss)

This very brief tutorial mission is designed to get you accustomed to the controls and basic gameplay functions. Thing starts off on a quiet end of the destroyed Brooklyn Bridge and must work to the opposite end to the Bridge arena where he meets the boss character.

Get a feel for the controls and move along the bridge to where you have to jump across the platform. Then use the attack button to break through the debris barrier before continuing. Note the cutscene and the introduction of your first opponent. These are Invaders—the grunts of the alien forces that you fight all the way through Story mode. Clobber four Invaders in this next short section before you move on. These peons are quite easy; throw cars at them for quick deaths. When you're done with them, move up to the high bridge section and smash through the rock barrier on the right to access the boss.

This brute is really a Decapitator, a later enemy type that you see a lot of throughout the story. There is nothing too challenging about this fight aside from the fact that he'll toss cars at you. This is a great time to practice catching thrown objects; just tap the throw button prior to impact and you should catch the object safely. One solid car hit is nearly all it takes to eliminate this alien boss.

Tip

This mission unlocks the Wolverine plotline.

Note

Throughout Story mode, you come across several tutorials, explaining everything from jumping attacks to super throws. Usually that skill is immediately relevant to the mission at hand to give you ample time to practice.

It's On Now

Location: Brooklyn Bridge

Opponents: Invaders

Thing's second mission is a bit more challenging, with more Invaders showing up to hamper your progress. Thing starts off in the Bridge arena, where you must kick the butts of a handful of Invaders. Once this is complete, a helicopter crashes into the side of the arena and opens a passageway through the debris.

Move into the now-open passage and find a couple of Invaders rushing to attack. When they're done with, move ahead to the platform with the car, and use it to crush the handful of Invaders attacking from here and the high platform. One exploding car is enough to take out most of them if they're in a group. Jump across to the other side of the bridge and note all the cars available—time to wreak some havoc! Two small waves of Invaders attack on this side. Swat and throw cars at them all to make quick work of this level.

CATCH THIS!

Location: New York Streets
Opponents: Invaders, Decapitators

Thing starts this mission in a short alley. The Decapitator behind the force field is milling about, ready to pick up an object to throw at you. Your first objective is to catch the things he's hurling at you and use them to destroy the Turlin Engine to your left—destroying the engine deactivates the force field. It may take a few throws to complete, but once the field is off, you can go in and finish off the Decapitator.

Now break through the debris barrier in the next alley to access the main part of the level, which is an isolated street section. Watch for a Decapitator to throw objects down the alley at you before you reach the open street. Peek out into the street and lure the opponents back into the narrow alley to deal with one at a time—out in the open it's much more difficult to avoid flying objects and weapons coming from multiple directions. Deal with several Decapitators and then another wave of Invaders. If they are grouped, use super combo attacks with the shockwave effect to take them out quickly. Don't let them surround you or they'll pick you off like a school of piranhas.

When this group is destroyed, punch through the second debris barrier in the far alley and lure out the two Decapitators carrying garbage bins. Stay clear of their throws or they'll defeat you very quickly. Juggling and super air tackles work well against these bladed foes. Once these two are dealt with, you face a small final wave of Invaders before clearing the level.

CLOBBER 'EM ALL!

Objective: Defeat all enemies within two minutes!
Location: The Bridge
Opponents: Invaders, Decapitators, Ravagers

TIP

Make sure you're facing your opponents when swatting objects toward them.

The first bonus stage is set in the Bridge arena. This is a tough fight if you try to eliminate every one of the 13 opponents individually! This is critical—you must take advantage of Thing's strength and swat every object available at your opponents to cause impact damage and chain reaction explosions. If you're lucky enough to have aliens in a group, feel free to use super combo shockwave attacks, but swatting objects is definitely the best way to go. Be cautious of the new opponents (Ravagers) that have an energy beam weapon to use against you from a distance.

CAUTION

Avoid going into Rage mode if you're low on time.

broken things

Objective: Defeat all enemies while wounded!
Location: NYC Streets
Opponents: Invaders, Decapitators, Ravagers

tip

Use object attacks to raise Thing's rage meter the fastest. You need the extra boost from Rage mode to kick butt in this bonus mission.

This bonus mission takes place in the NYC Streets arena. Thing begins with half strength, so you must fight at peak efficiency to get through this bonus round. The first wave is the most difficult (several Decapitators). Dodge the cars they throw and take them out quickly with juggling attacks that link into super air tackles. The next wave of Invaders is easier to eliminate with a few explosions from thrown or swatted cars. Due to the arena's enclosed nature and small size, explosions are very effective. The last wave consists of several Ravagers who may lurk by the arena walls, so move around looking for them or they'll blast you from apparently out of nowhere.

caution

The Decapitators can throw cars at you—one hit and you're dead! Eliminate them quickly to avoid this fatal hazard.

thing: sacrifice

Objective: Fault Zone must defeat Thing!
Location: NYC Streets

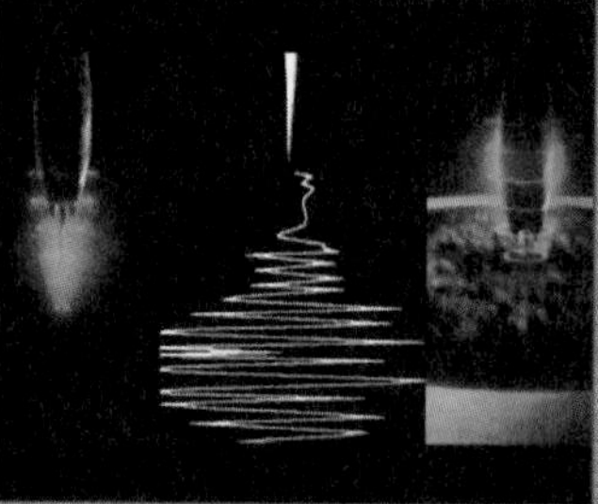

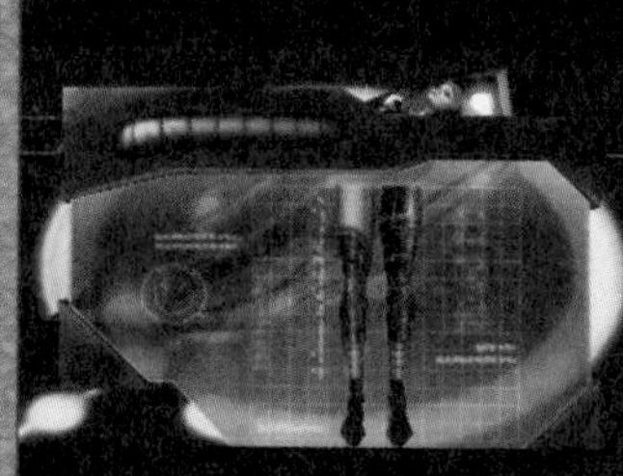

Take control of the Imperfects' stunning little dancer: Fault Zone. You must defeat Thing in the streets of NYC—an arena packed with weapons and objects for him to use against you. The key to success here is to use your high mobility to its full potential. Literally dance circles around Thing so he can't target you with wielded weapons, thrown cars, and the many swatted objects that will be rifling at you through the air. Use her quick mobility to get in fast, strike hard with super combos, and get out before Thing grabs you. Whittle him down using a hit-and-run approach. Don't bother trying to throw objects at him; Thing catches or redirects nearly everything coming his way.

Wolverine

dead end, destroy a few Invaders and a Decapitator to end the mission. Wall attacks are very effective in the close quarters of this dead-end alley.

Street Fight

Location: NYC Streets
Opponents: Invaders, Decapitators

Wolverine begins his journey in a NYC back alley populated by a small army of Invaders—this should be a cake walk for our ferocious and furry little friend. Most of the mission you'll fight Invaders. They aren't much of a challenge for Logan. Regular and super attack combos that link into air tackles are usually enough to take out most peons. Fight through the alley and the handful of Invaders. Logan is much faster than Thing, so it may take a bit of getting used to compared to the previous missions.

Tip

Use Logan's quickness to your advantage: execute many wall-running attacks from different angles to keep your opponents off balance.

Dice up a large wave of Invaders once you've cleared the path into the main street section. Out in the open there is more danger of object attacks from Invaders—they can throw only Class 1 objects, but they're still a threat. When you've defeated the street wave of foes, the force field blocking the far alley deactivates, and you can proceed into the next alley section. Wall run (mobility move) over the flames to get to the far side. In the

House Party

Location: Avengers' Mansion
Opponents: Invaders, Marauders

Tip

Air tackles work much better against flying opponents than air attacks.

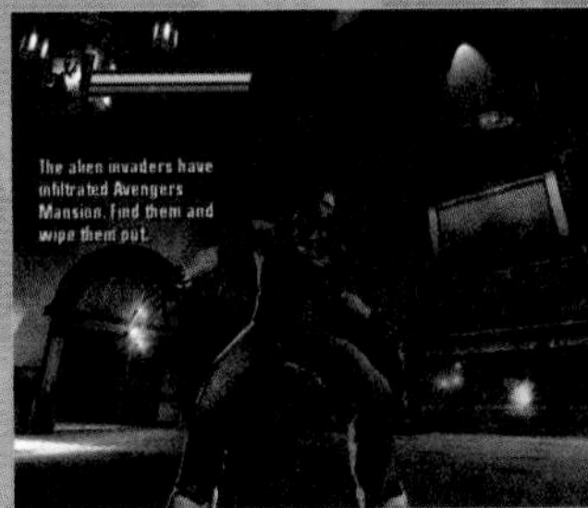

Logan starts this mission in the entry to the Avengers' Mansion. All is quiet for now, but the chaos begins soon enough. Move out into the hall and assess the two sets of security laser grids. Wall run on the side with the opening over the first grid, pause in the middle, then again over the second grid. Go through the far door into the arena and the fight starts. The first wave of Invaders shouldn't pose too much of a problem. Wolvie has tons of room to move and launch wall attacks.

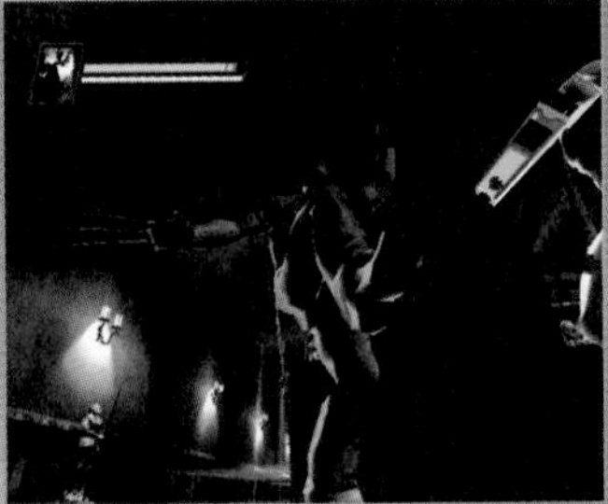

When the second wave attacks with the Invaders and flying Marauders, things get more interesting. Ignore the Invaders while eliminating the threat of the flying droids, because you need to worry about their ranged energy weapons. Air tackles and super air tackles work wonders against Marauders. Once they're destroyed, finish off the last wave of Invaders to end the mission.

Note

There may be some straggler Invaders in the far hall. Check this area if the level doesn't end.

Femme Fatale

Objective: Wolverine must defeat The Wink!
Location: Avengers' Mansion Basement

A mysterious woman is in the basement of the Avengers' Mansion going through the computer. Find out what she's up to!

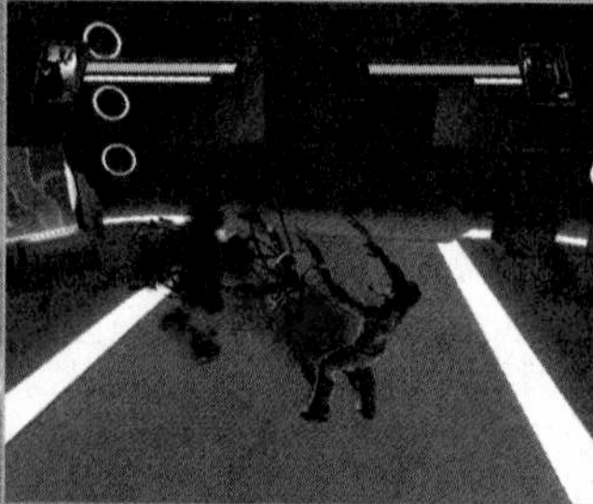

Once you make contact, The Wink attacks without hesitation. She teleports often, so it can be hard to pin her down in one location for long. When this happens, wait for her to be solid for a few moments and then resume your attack.

Tip

The Wink is temporarily invincible when teleporting. Dodge her teleporting attacks and counter with combos when she is solid.

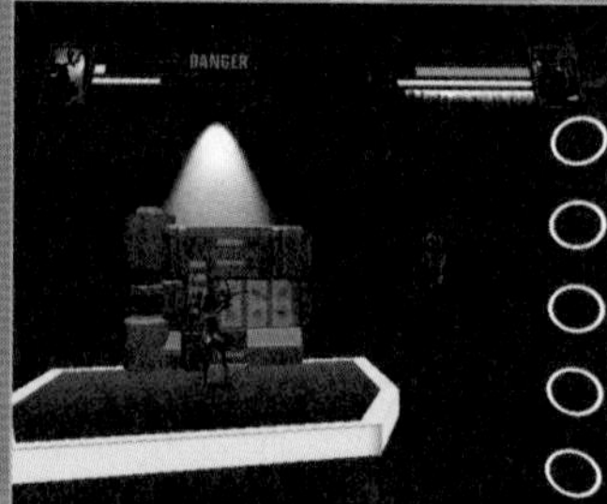

As you damage her, The Wink intermittently teleports to the top four platforms to throw barrels down at you. Dodge or jump to avoid these impacts and possible explosions. Look for the poles lying in the arena corners to throw up at her, or just wait for her to throw the last barrel, then she goes back up to the computer platform to continue her research. You must get up there to attack her—climb up and jump attack her from the wall. Repeat this as often as it takes to end The Wink's magic show. When she's finally sliced 'n' diced, you get a clue to the chaos that's going on in NYC.

Caution

When you knock The Wink down, don't stand over her—her rising attack is quite powerful and easily chains into a combo. Instead, nail her with some thrown barrels or wielded poles.

Claws of Fury

Objective: Defeat all enemies in three minutes!
Location: The Bridge
Opponents: Invaders, Maulers, Eviscerators

Is Wolvie up for the task? Of course he is! The official spokesperson for hack 'n' slash is about to test his mettle on two new alien military units: Maulers and Eviscerators. Maulers have a shockwave attack; watch for it shortly after they plant both claws in the ground. Eviscerators have an energized bear-hug attack that they execute when in close.

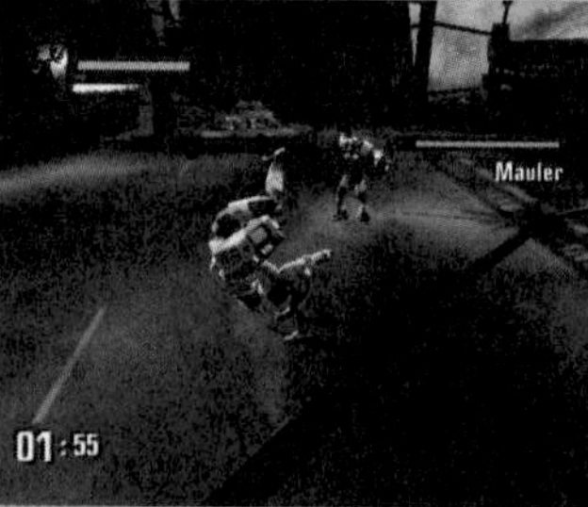

First off, deal with a handful of Invaders. Be quick about using all the nearby barrels to take out the group of them in fiery explosions. When they're down, a couple Maulers appear. These guys are tough, so use super combo attacks and juggles to get them up into the air and link into super air tackles.

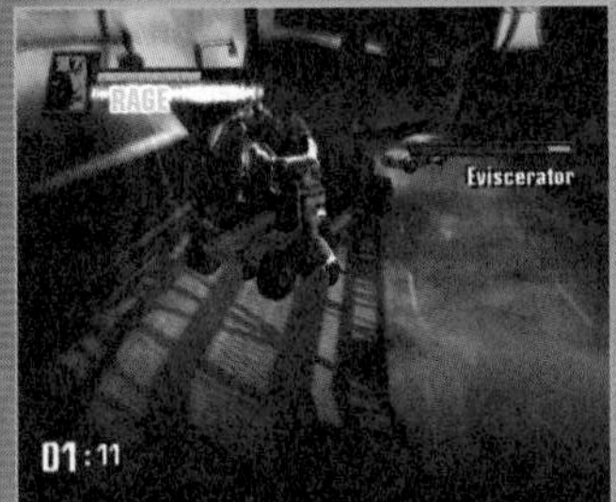

Several Eviscerators comprise the third wave. They're not that tough, but limit the time you spend in close with them because their clutching attack does moderate damage. Keep them at bay with objects and mobility attacks. The last small wave is a mix of all three units, so your tactics will vary according to which individual you're facing. If you made good time eliminating the first wave of Invaders, you should have ample time to deal with this last wave.

To Defy a Goddess

Objective: Wolverine must defeat Altered Storm!
Location: The Bridge

This battle is fairly straightforward, but that doesn't mean it's going to be easy. Storm is often underrated in combat, but you're about to learn just how dangerous a goddess can be. Storm doesn't have any fancy AI behavior (not that she needs any help), and she just wants to kick your butt. Familiarize yourself with the AI Storm in the Marvel Heroes section, as the same strategy applies here. She is highly mobile in this arena and spends a lot of time in the air. Consequently, use air tackles and super air tackles often to bring her back down to ground level and hopefully you can get close enough to grab her.

As soon as the fight starts, she tries nailing you with her ranged lightning attacks—get moving! Dodge, run, do whatever you have to do. If you stand still, that's all she needs for a lock and then the lighting strikes. If she can see you, she can hit you; look for objects or terrain to put between you and her to avoid being shocked or to act as a lightning rod. Use the barrels scattered around the arena to whittle her down. She'll catch a few of them but just keep throwing. When the explosions start she'll take some high damage. Mix it up by taking the fight in close so she can't use her lighting attacks. Use super combo attacks but don't stress too much about juggling. Storm has an excellent air recovery move that she'll often use before you can air tackle her. In close combat, Wolverine should be able to finish her off.

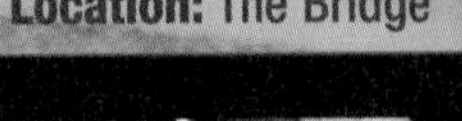

Wolverine: Sacrifice

Objective: Brigade must defeat Wolverine!
Location: The Bridge

Meet Brigade, the true firepower of the Imperfects. This Frankenstein war machine is literally a one-man army! There's no reason why Brigade shouldn't blast Wolverine right off the bridge. Use super jump attacks, throw cars and the semi, and fire off some cannon blasts to pop that little fur ball a good one! Wolvie can't catch cars, so that's almost a fail-safe attack, but he can still super block if he's got the SP. If you can keep Logan at a distance, this one should be in the bag!

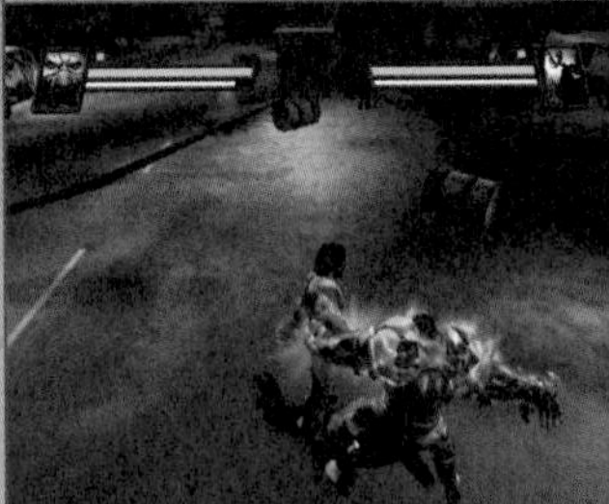

Tip

Remember to use Brigade's rapid fire ability—mash the attack button to fire quickly but watch your SP meter! You don't want to expend fully and be temporarily out of commission during a seizure. If you get into Rage mode, get your guns off and blow Wolverine away!

Elektra

Death from Afar

Location: NYC Streets
Opponents: Invaders, Ravagers

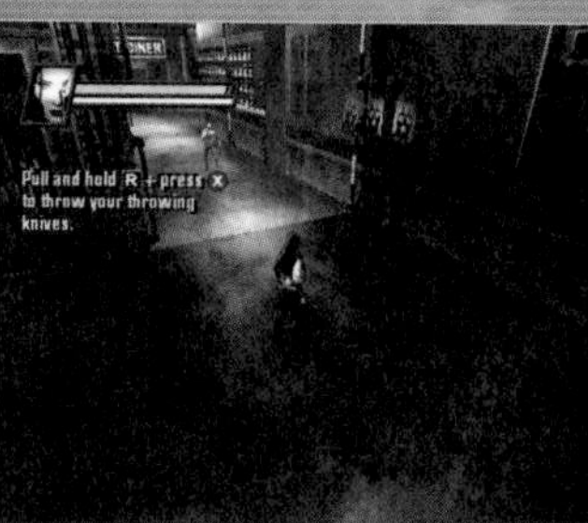

Elektra is the undisputed queen of assassins. Work through the NYC street sections, starting in the familiar back alley. Use far attacks with her sais to kill the first Ravager through the force field. When it drops, move ahead to repeat the sequence. A couple waves of Invaders and Ravagers spawn in the open street section ahead. Lure them all back to the alley and kill them one by one with ranged attacks and wall-run attacks. The Ravagers' energy weapons are far too dangerous out in the open. When the street waves are clear, super block a Ravager's blast upon him to drop the far force field and end the mission.

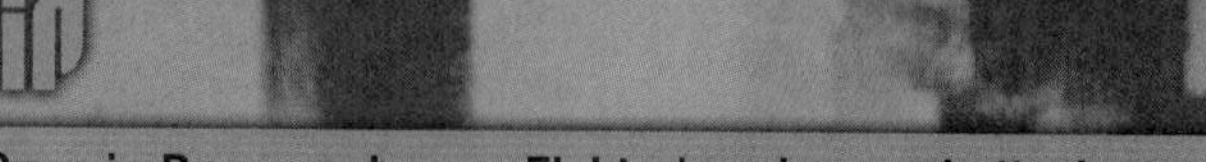

Once in Rage mode, use Elektra's sai ranged attacks to quickly kill Invaders and Ravagers.

Top of the World

Location: NYC Rooftops
Opponents: Invaders, Marauders

Up above the city, things get a bit more interesting. You can easily fall or be blown right off the rooftops, so watch your step—especially when fighting Marauders. Pay close attention to where the air-conditioner units are. Throw them all at your enemies so none are lying around to explode and knock you off the roof. Proceed across the rooftops by wall running over the gaps between buildings. When the Marauders attack, deal with them first—air tackles work best! Then clean up the remaining riffraff. It's possible to kill most of your opponents by throwing air conditioners across to the next buildings. Head through the hole in the wall near the fuel containers and eliminate the few Invaders guarding the Turlin Engine. Destroy the machine to complete the mission.

You can destroy the machine from a distance by object attacks, so save the air conditioners for this purpose and end the mission from a distance.

Daredevil

Objective: Elektra must defeat Altered Daredevil!
Location: *Daily Bugle*

Something is wrong with Daredevil: he's not feeling himself! Good ole blind justice can be a pain in the neck if you're not quick with your attacks. Daredevil is tough because he's so mobile; don't try attacking him in the air. Wait until he's on the ground—bring him down by hiding behind objects and waiting for him to come after you. An easy way to take him down is to throw objects at him, which he usually catches. But while he's preparing to throw them back at you, hit him hard with some ranged sai attacks. Hopefully that will cause subsequent explosions to damage him even more. Repeat this tactic as necessary. You can try to beat him down hand to hand, but Elektra and Daredevil are fairly evenly matched in fighting skills so it can go either way. If you go this route, use juggling combos that can be linked into air tackles.

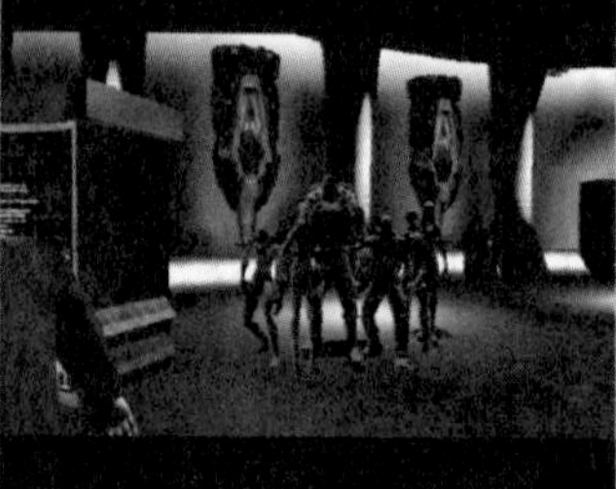

SILENT DEATH

Objective: Defeat 15 enemies!
Location: Avengers' Mansion
Opponents: Invaders, Decapitators, Ravagers

The key to completing this mission is to take your time. There is no time limit, only the objective of eliminating 15 enemies. You deal with a mix, so don't fight them with the same blanket strategy. Take out Invaders and Ravagers with either ranged sai attacks or attack combos with an air tackle. Decapitators are more difficult to defeat with hand-to-hand combos, so mix it up with super wall attacks and jumping techniques, and definitely take advantage of all the objects and weapons lying around.

TIP: Use Elektra's super wall attacks to deal the death blows in this arena. She can cover a lot of ground when using this technique—even hitting enemies almost halfway across the arena! This also helps to keep her mobile enough to avoid the Ravager's energy shots.

ASSASSIN'S BLADES

Objective: Destroy all the computer screens in the lab in 1 minute, 20 seconds!
Location: Avengers' Mansion Basement
Opponents: Invaders, Marauders

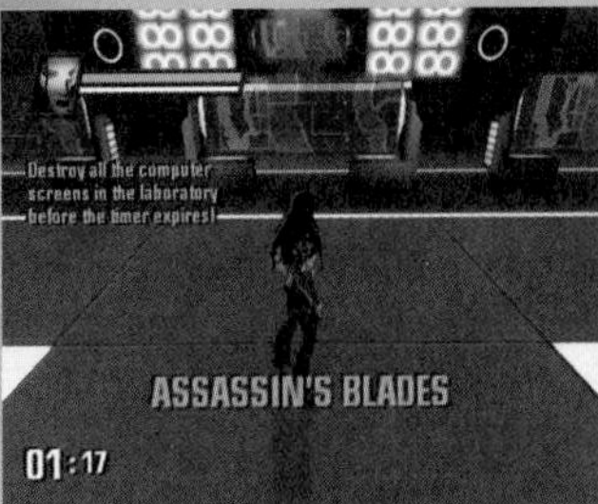

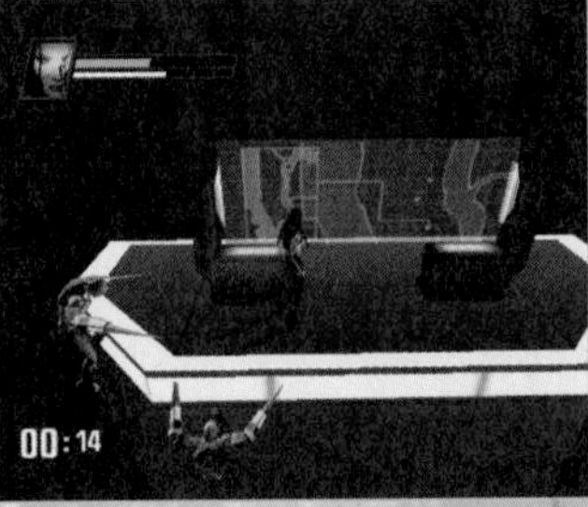

This bonus level is either really hard or really easy, depending how much time you waste playing it safe. The higher the risk, the higher the reward! To make quick work of this mission, ignore all opponents and go right for the screens! Systematically destroy all computer screens at ground level. When you're done, wall run up to one of the higher platforms, destroy the screen with a mobility attack (kick), which may then bust a piece of the screen bracket off and send it flying into the next platform along the wall, breaking it as well. Done correctly, you may only have to destroy half the screens on the upper levels.

TIP: Wall run from high platform to high platform—don't go back down to ground level once you're up there! With this tactic, you should complete the mission with ample time to spare.

ELEKTRA: SACRIFICE

Objective: The Wink must defeat Elektra!
Location: Power Plant Arena

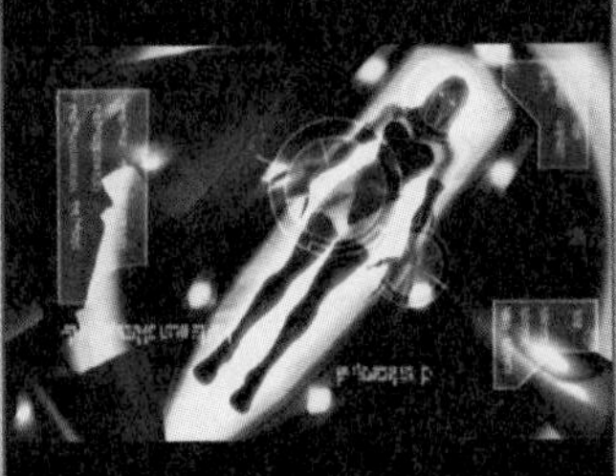

Now you see her, now you don't. The Wink is the Imperfects' resident magician/teleporter. Misdirection and surprise are her allies; use her teleportation ability to augment her attacks and keep Elektra moving in the wrong direction. Elektra may block many of your super attacks. If this happens, rely more on mobility, rising, and stomp attacks to defeat her.

CAUTION: Expect many long-range Kunai attacks from Elektra. Use your dodging teleport (rather than the mobility move version) to avoid using up your SP meter.

TIP: Super stomp attacks do incredible damage to Elektra.

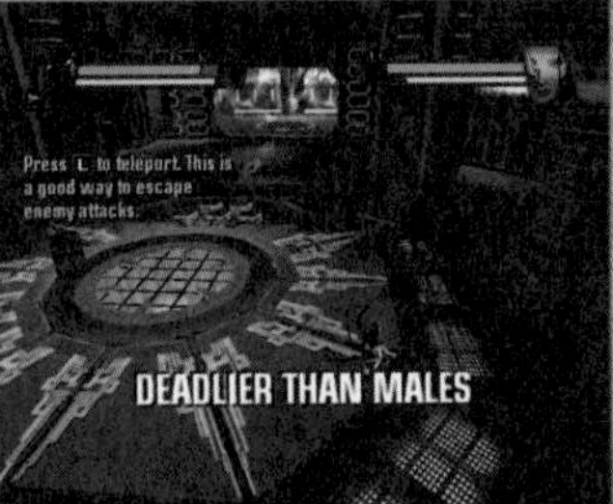

Daredevil

Redemption

Location: NYC Rooftops
Opponents: Invaders, Decapitators

High on the rooftop of the *Daily Bugle*, Daredevil starts his first mission. Practice swinging around and then head through the *Daily Bugle* sign to the rooftops below. There you find a mix of Invaders and Decapitators waiting for you in waves on each of the roofs. Mobility attacks, both swinging and running, work very well against both types of foes, but mix in super far attacks with your billy club too.

An effective alternate strategy is to use all of the objects you can to clear off the next rooftop over before you progress. Once you get to the last roof, eliminate a couple waves of Decapitators. You may have to back off and retreat to the previous roof to regroup before coming at them again with a full SP meter.

Tip

If you need a break to recharge your SP meter, wall run up to the top of the wall near the large fuel containers. You can hang out up top where your enemies can't reach you. Watch for the odd flying air conditioner, however!

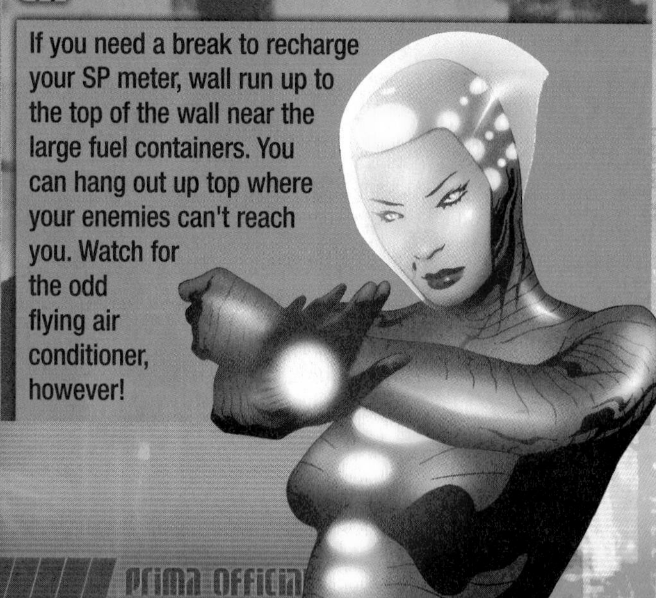

Scorched Earth

Objective: Defeat all opponents in six minutes!
Location: Grand Central Station
Opponents: Invaders, Eviscerators

Aliens have planted explosives all around Grand Central Station. Daredevil must defeat all the aliens in less than six minutes to thwart their plans. Most of this level is filled with Invaders, with a handful of Eviscerators scattered around trying to grab you. Eliminate all the Invaders in the first wave. Once the Eviscerators appear at the cutscene, you're about halfway finished.

Go back and forth from the ground floor to around the second level pillars to ensure that all enemies are eliminated. There are several nooks and crannies on both levels where aliens can be missed, so search the entire area thoroughly to get them all.

Tip

If the timer is still ticking down and you think you got everyone, head up to the top level and check for stragglers behind one of the walls or pillars.

The Electric Man

Objective: Daredevil must defeat Johnny Ohm!
Location: Grand Central Station

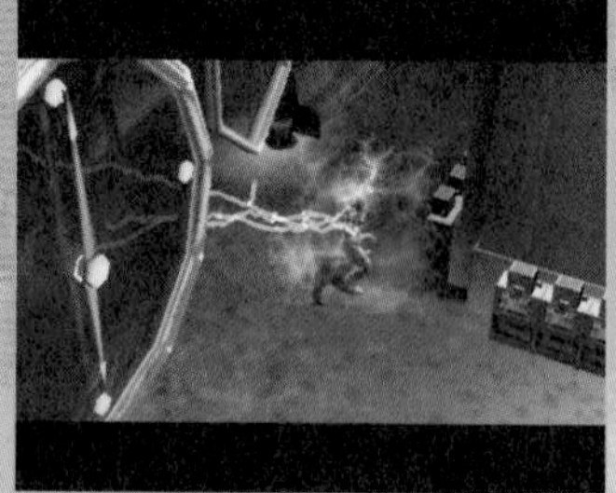

Johnny Ohm draws his power from the clock in the arena's center. Dodge his lightning attacks and throw objects at the clock to destroy it before trying to take on Ohm. He throws a lot of ranged lightning attacks your way in the beginning, but once you destroy the clock, his SP will be much more limited.

If you can keep him at a distance while his SP meter is too low for him to use lightning, it's very easy to beat him down. Throw objects at him and use mobility attacks to quickly move in and out in a hit-and-run style.

Tip

Watch Johnny's SP meter: his ranged lightning attacks are powerful, but they take up a lot of juice. If he's low, then it's time to hit him hard from a distance!

Note

Destroying the clock is optional, but it does make Johnny Ohm weaker.

Take Them Down

Objective: Defeat 20 enemies!
Location: The Bridge
Opponents: Invaders, Decapitators, Eviscerators, Desolators

As intimidating as this mix of alien adversaries can be, there is an easy way to get your 20 kills—and it's not standing around in the open being swarmed from all sides. You must contend with a threatening mix of ground soldiers and flying Desolator droids in this bonus mission.

Tip

The Desolators are easily destroyed by super air tackles.

First off, get out of the arena's middle and up to the high ground of the middle walkway. Up top, you can wait until the enemy comes to you; this tactic also limits how many of them you have to deal with at one time. If you're getting swarmed even up on the walkway, put the structure between you and your opponents while you pick and choose who to fight. Many new waves of enemies spawn to keep your options open, so feel free to just keep swatting them off the walkway until you reach your 20. There's no time limit, so sit back and let the butt kicking begin.

Tip

The Decapitators are the hardest to kill in this mission. You can ignore them and take out the other alien units with less effort.

Lover's Quarrel

Objective: Daredevil must defeat Altered Elektra while poisoned!
Location: NYC Streets

This bonus mission starts with you down health already! Elektra's poisoned throwing dagger found its mark. Your time is limited, so don't waste it! Altered Elektra is resistant to some physical attacks. Super throws don't faze her much, but use them to get her off her feet for a moment while you hit her with some thrown barrels or metal bins. Object attacks work very well against her; make them your primary tactic.

Daredevil: Sacrifice

Objective: Solara must defeat Daredevil!
Location: NYC Streets

For someone engulfed in solar fire, Solara is very cool. She's got flame attacks similar to Human Torch and the fighting skills of Elektra. Solara is also one of the few characters who can execute four-hit combos. For a four-hit combo against Daredevil, use attacks in this order: normal attack, normal attack, super attack combo, and full super attack combo, to deal out excessive damage. Don't expend your SP on flying; instead save it for ranged fire attacks. If Daredevil spends a lot of time swinging around, hover near him long enough to get a super air tackle. This should be an easy win for the Imperfects.

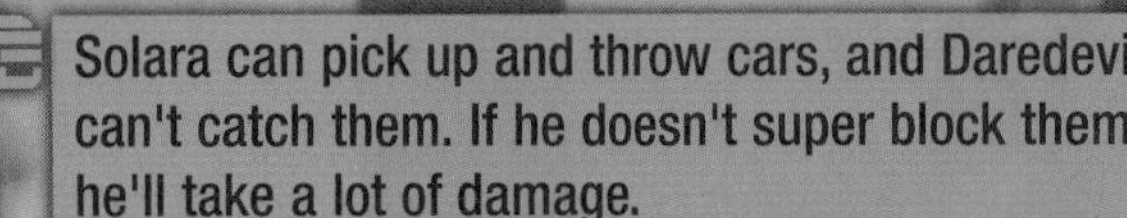

Tip: Solara can pick up and throw cars, and Daredevil can't catch them. If he doesn't super block them, he'll take a lot of damage.

Tip: Always use Solara's super rising attack as a backup after getting knocked down—it's a high-damage technique.

Return Home

Objective: Destroy the Turlin Engines!
Location: The Bridge
Opponents: Invaders, Ravagers, Desolators

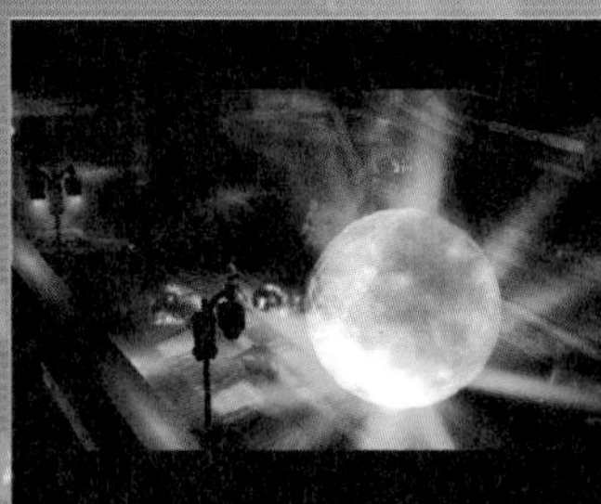

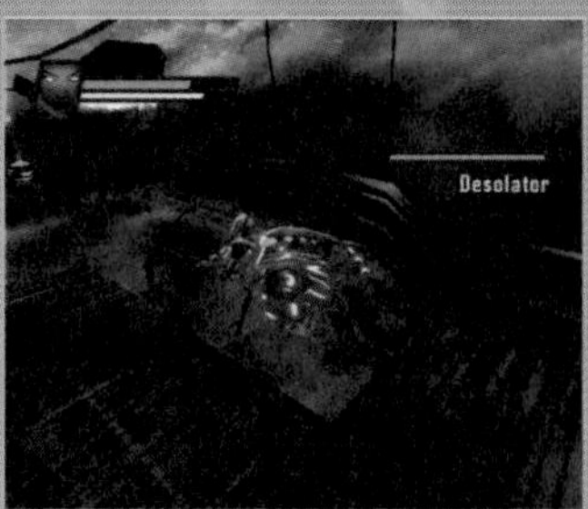

This level starts with you going one direction then working back the way you came. First off, head toward the first Turlin Engine and destroy the first wave of enemies. There are Intruders and Desolators initially, and then two Ravagers to deal with. Destroy the Turlin Engine with hovering lighting attacks, and watch for two more Ravagers to show up immediately.

Eliminate the Ravagers and fly back in the direction you came from. Fly high up and over the first force field, and take out the Intruders, Desolators, and Ravagers that appear in this middle area. Then fly high over the second force field and into the main arena. Fight from the raised walkway in the middle. It's easy to limit your opponents here and it makes a nice platform to jump from to air tackle the many Desolators flying around. Keep moving and destroying the Desolators while avoiding fire from the few Ravagers on the ground. When you've got a few moments to spare, use ranged lightning attacks on the Turlin Engine to destroy it and end the mission.

Tip

Save your ranged lightning attacks for Ravagers, because it seems to do them the most damage.

House Call

Location: Avengers' Mansion
Opponents: Invaders, Desolators

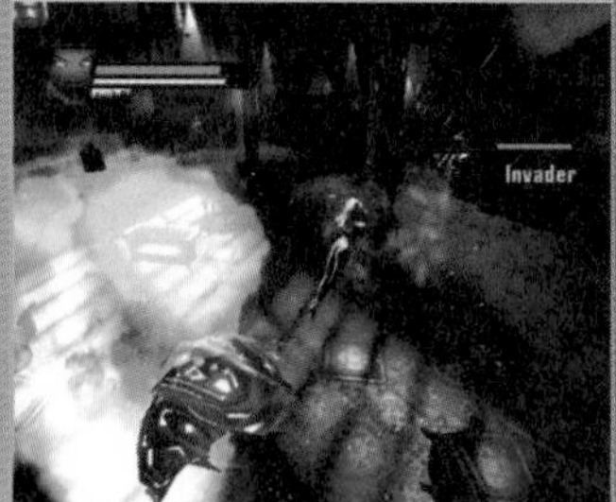

This is a very simple mission. Storm starts in the entryway of the Avengers' Mansion, where a small wave of Invaders appears to halt your progress. Kill them with objects and melee attacks before heading out into the hallway. Hover over the two sets of laser grids down the hall and into the main arena. Here you must destroy another wave of Invaders and Desolators. Use super throws and attack combos on the Invaders and super air tackles on the Desolators. Chalk up another easy win for the Marvel heroes.

Tip

Invaders don't catch objects very well, so use the tons of objects lying around the mansion as weapons.

Earthquake!

Objective: Storm must defeat Fault Zone!
Location: The Bridge

This can be a tricky mission to complete the first couple times around—don't underestimate the Imperfects' little waif Fault Zone. She fights for a while and then runs to one of the two rubble areas to use her special shockwave attacks. When she does this you have two choices: run for cover behind the bridge, or use your ranged lighting attacks to shock her into submission. The boulders that come flying out of the rubble piles move quickly and cause impact damage—avoid those at all costs!

Fault Zone is a very localized fighter. Storm should have no problem defeating her at a distance with thrown objects and super mobility attacks (Ball Lightning).

FIGHT TO SURVIVE

Objective: Defeat 15 enemies with a ring out!
Location: Grand Central Station
Opponents: Invaders, Ravagers

Right off the bat for this bonus mission, note that the regular barriers to the ring-out area have been removed. This is a very easy bonus mission if you stick with one tried and tested technique—use only Storm's super throw! It's all you really need to win.

Always face the ring-out area, and move only to position an enemy directly between you and the edge. Using this technique, you should be able to supply the ring-out pit with a continuous supply of alien enemies.

You may need to dodge fire from the Ravagers at times. Keep an eye out for them, and if possible, send them into the pit first.

WRATH OF ELEMENTS

Objective: Defeat all enemies!
Location: *Daily Bugle*
Opponents: Invaders, Ravagers, Desolators

On the rooftop of the *Daily Bugle*, you face several waves of alien troops—but nothing you haven't seen before. Wreak havoc with the host of objects lying around: barrels, pipes, air conditioners. Eliminate Invaders with object attacks, Desolators with air tackles, and Ravagers with super mobility attacks (Ball Lighting) to make the most efficient use of your skills.

STORM: SACRIFICE

Objective: Altered Wolverine must defeat Storm!
Location: Van Roekel's Headquarters

Dodge, dodge, dodge—those are our three best words of advice. Storm will call down lightning strike after lightning strike until her SP meter is low. Van Roekel's Headquarters contains no shortage of objects to throw at Storm, and that's exactly what you should do. Weaken her with object attacks, and go in for the kill with super attack combos. If you're lucky you may get an air tackle in, but Storm is usually quick enough to pull off her air recovery move.

If Storm goes for the recharging module in the circle to replenish her health, knock her out of the air with an object attack.

Venom

The Pit

Location: Avengers' Mansion
Opponents: Invaders, Decapitators, Desolators

The fight begins in the entry hall of the Avengers' Mansion. Venom must first destroy a wave of Invaders (Web Bullets work wonders) before moving down the hallway toward the main arena. Inside the large open area, another wave of aliens spawns with a host of Decapitators and Desolators. Use air tackles against the flying droids. Web Bullets and mobility attacks (Corkscrew Kicks from off the zipline) work well against the Decapitators.

Seek and Devour

Objective: Destroy 30 enemies!
Location: The Bridge
Opponents: Decapitators, Marauders, Maulers

Venom must fight along the bridge through a horde of Decapitators and Marauders. The Turlin Engines scattered around the area give off a special energy that Venom's symbiote can absorb for healing. Save them for when you need them, however, as you must work through many opponents in this mission.

Air tackle Marauders for easy kills, and eliminate Decapitators with a mix of Web Bullets, thrown cars, and juggling attacks. Once you've defeated approximately 25 enemies, the Maulers show up in one last wave. These aliens are not that mobile, so they make great targets for Web Bullets. Try to lure them up onto the walkway in the arena, with their backs to the ring-out area. Blast them with a Web Bullet, which should knock them backward, and if the trajectory is good they'll be knocked right out of the arena for an easy last couple kills.

Tip

Destroy the Turlin Engines and absorb their healing energy!

Fatal Heat

Objective: Venom must defeat Solara!
Location: Power Plant

Considering Venom's inherent aversion and weakness to fire, this can be a challenging mission. Solara has a several opportunities to heal herself using the fuel pipes coming out of the walls. When she approaches them and causes them to explode, the flames engulf her and heal the damage you've caused. The best way around this is to do as much damage to her as quickly as possible. Throw everything you can get your webs on. The huge chunks of pillars that remain after they're broken are hard-hitting weapons—use them to put out Solara's flames.

Tip

Swat or throw the large Tesla Coils at Solara to cause high damage.

Caution

Venom is very susceptible to fire damage; stay mobile in this fight to avoid her long-range flame attacks!

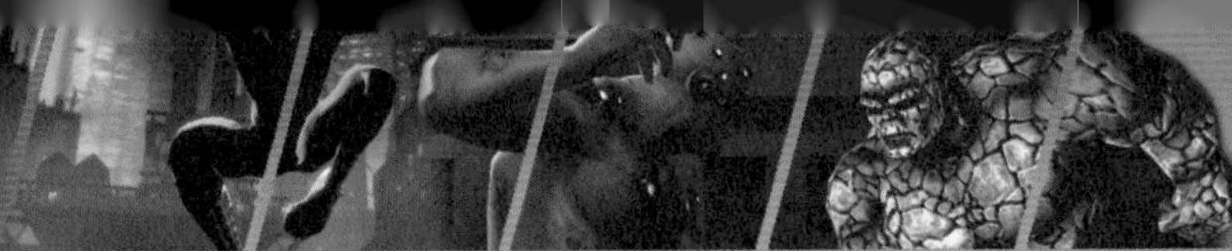

WANTON DESTRUCTION

Objective: Destroy 35 objects in three minutes!
Location: NYC Streets
Opponents: Invaders, Decapitators, Marauders

This bonus mission is complete and utter carnage, just the way Venom likes it. It's almost like a shopping spree, but you get to blow things up! Venom has three minutes in the NYC Streets arena to wreck as much as he can—cars, poles, newspaper boxes, it's all fair game. Just keep moving, swatting objects, and avoiding the enemies altogether; you don't need to distract yourself by fighting them.

TIP

Swatting or throwing cars and the resulting explosions usually destroys multiple objects.

RISE AND FALL

Objective: Defeat 12 opponents with a ring out!
Location: *Daily Bugle*
Opponents: Eviscerators, Ravagers

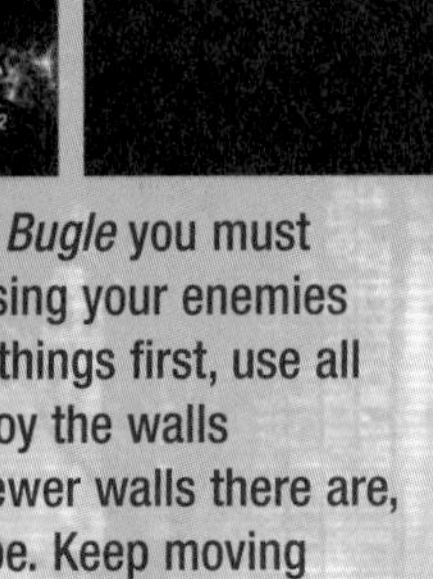

From the rooftop of the *Daily Bugle* you must complete 12 ring outs by tossing your enemies into the mist below. But first things first, use all the objects available to destroy the walls surrounding the arena. The fewer walls there are, the easier your mission will be. Keep moving around the arena so the Ravagers can't hit you with their energy weapons. Once the walls are cleared away, use Web Bullets and normal and super throws to quickly score ring outs.

TIP

A few swats with one of the large radio towers usually destroys the *Daily Bugle* sign.

TIP

Web Bullets, normal throws (facing the ring out), and super throws (with your back to the ring out) are the best ways to toss enemies off the rooftop.

VENOM: SACRIFICE

Objective: Hazmat must defeat Venom!
Location: Grand Central Station

Hazmat is the toxic swinger of the Imperfects—he's highly mobile and dangerous at long range. Use these traits to defeat Venom with a bit of his own medicine. Venom and Hazmat have very similar fighting styles, and similar downfalls. Both fighters are not very technical in close, both have ranged attacks, and both are highly mobile.

Hurl the concrete blocks littering the arena at Venom. If he manages to catch them, use your long-range toxic-ooze attacks. This is a close matchup; use all the environmental features here to get the drop on Venom.

TIP

Remember that Hazmat has a long-distance zipline-grab ability just like Spider-Man and Venom. Use the zipline to quickly grab objects and throw them at your foes.

SPIDER-MAN

SPIDER-MAN!

Objective: Destroy the 11 computer consoles!
Location: Power Plant
Opponents: Eviscerators, Desolators

Spider-Man's first mission is a quick destruction job. Like other similar missions, you can complete this level faster if you ignore the alien military units, and just concentrate on destroying the computer consoles. Normal attacks work well against the consoles. Don't forget the ones on the upper level.

AIRLIFT

Objective: Defend both helicopters, defeat all enemies!
Location: NYC Streets
Opponents: Invaders, Marauders

This mission is very objective oriented, with two phases. You must protect two rescue helicopters (one at a time) from attacking alien hordes. As the mission starts, head over to the first chopper and keep all the Invaders away from it. There are a few Marauders in the mix as well; as with any flying droid, air tackles work wonders against them.

After the cutscene, head across to the second chopper to protect it from another wave of Invaders and a few more Marauders. This is a straightforward fight as long as you don't get surrounded by alien units or let the Invaders stand around attacking the helicopters.

DEADLY VENOM

Objective: Spider-Man must defeat Altered Venom!
Location: *Daily Bugle*

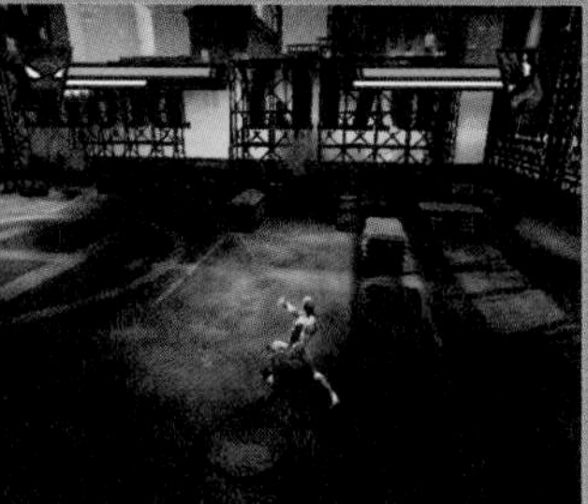

The rooftop of the *Daily Bugle* is an appropriate place for this showdown. Venom is not feeling himself and he's out for Spidey's blood. These two are very evenly matched, so it comes down to who has a better plan—and it better be you!

Venom can be a pain because he blocks very well, so you need to disturb his rhythm to score some big damage. Throw objects, blast him with Web Bullets, and always use rising attacks. Normal and super attack combos that juggle into air attacks work well if he doesn't pull off an air recovery.

CAUTION

Be very cautious if Venom picks up the large fuel containers; they do a lot of damage.

WARPED EVIL

Objective: Spider-Man must defeat Altered Hazmat!
Location: The Bridge

This battle is very evenly matched between fighters. Hazmat may be altered but he still has the same attacks as regular old Hazmat. Use the zipline to grab objects from a distance and keep throwing them his way. A direct hit with a car does a lot of damage. In melee combat, Spider-Man has much better technical fighting ability than Hazmat, so put your normal and super attack combos to work! Don't feel compelled to include juggling techniques, as Hazmat can air recover quite well.

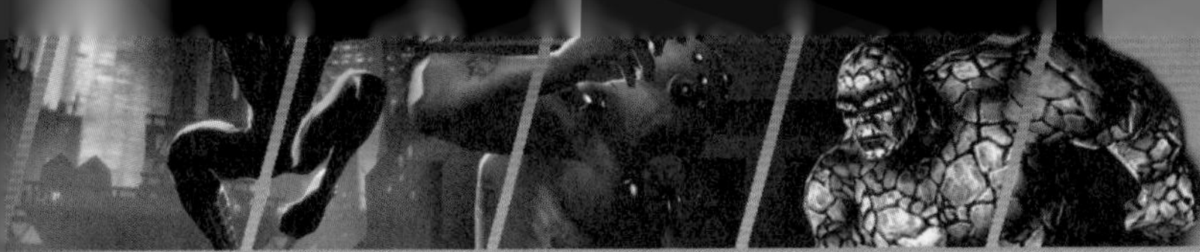

CAUTION

Watch for falling debris and rubble in this arena.

FRAGILE LIFE

Objective: Spider-Man must defeat all enemies!
Location: Grand Central Station
Opponents: Ravagers, Maulers, Predators

This bonus mission can provide quite a challenge if you fight the enemies on their own terms—they attempt to outmatch you with a strong cross section of offenses. The solid and challenging mix of aliens here has all bases covered: ground attacks, air attacks, and ranged attacks.

With this many Predators to deal with, you're going to spend a lot of time jumping and using air tackles against them. This helps you dodge fire from the Ravagers at the same time. Once you've eliminated the Predators, deal with the Ravagers: Web Bullets and attack combos work well against them. Maulers are the last part of the alien attack. Spidey is much more agile than they are—don't spend much time on the ground and their ground attacks can't touch you. Swing to the upper level and knock the Maulers off as they come up after you; the extra fall damage helps eliminate them faster.

CAUTION

Watch for the glowing mines left on the ground by the flying Predator droids.

NOTE

Your stamina does not regenerate in this mission.

SPIDER-MAN: SACRIFICE

Objective: Johnny Ohm must defeat Spider-Man!
Location: *Daily Bugle*

Johnny Ohm is more than a lightning rod. He's actually pulling his charge right out of the air around him. You must destroy that annoying bug Spider-Man any way possible.

The rooftop of the *Daily Bugle* is littered with objects to be used as weapons: pipes, barrels, and air conditioners. Use these objects often but with a built-in secondary attack to get past Spidey's blocks. If he blocks or catches your thrown objects, hit him right away with your ranged lightning attacks; ideally this will cause a subsequent explosion, adding more damage. Use your flight sparingly, just to get out of the way or to find more objects to throw. Save your SP meter for ranged lightning attacks. Alternately, if Spidey is swinging around often, hover for brief periods to take him down with super air tackles.

CAUTION

If you fight Spidey in close, beware of his super attack combos—they do a great deal of damage!

Human Torch

Field Trip to Hell

Objective: Destroy all Turlin Engines in four minutes!
Location: Grand Central Station
Opponents: Ravagers, Eviscerators, Marauders

Turlin Engines are scattered around Grand Central Station, supplying power to the alien forces. Torch must destroy all of them before time runs out. The one engine on the ground floor powers a force field that protects the others on the upper levels, so that one must be destroyed first.

Once the force field is down, you can access the upper levels to destroy the remaining engines. There are several ways to do this efficiently. Super attacks (Fireballs) work well but consume much of your SP meter. Normal jumping attacks work in a few hits, but must be placed properly to hit the levitating engines. Object attacks actually work very well. If you're using the last tactic, save your SP meter to get you around the arena to find objects then go back to your target engine.

Tip

You have to destroy only the engines, not the alien peons. You can ignore them if you wish.

Torchbearer

Location: Van Roekel's Headquarters
Opponents: Eviscerators, Ravagers, Maulers

This is one of the game's longest missions, so set a conservative pace. The long series of corridors in Van Roekel's Headquarters contains numerous objects and force fields to make things interesting.

As you progress down the hall, you are isolated inside pairs of force fields, making you square off against a wave of alien troops. The key to success is not staying put for too long. Keep moving and use mobility attacks and normal attack combos when you've run out of props to throw. Every once in a while throw in some ranged fire attacks to knock enemies back, but don't overdo it as these drain your SP meter quickly. When you come to the areas with the blue energy walls, put them between you and your enemies to limit how many of them you face at once. This is an excellent way to pick them off individually. Patience is key on this mission; if you rush through it you'll never see the end.

Tip

Air ram attacks work miracles in this level. If you can send your enemies flying a long way back, they take more falling damage. They take even more if they strike a wall before hitting the ground.

Caution

This is one of the longer missions in Story mode, so conserve your SP meter or recharge it often.

Old Friends

Objective: Human Torch must defeat Altered Thing!
Location: Van Roekel's Headquarters

Ben is being controlled by Van Roekel: this is one clobberin' time you can stand to avoid altogether! Regardless, you must beat Ben down to help rid him of the alien mind-control device.

The best way to get through this level is to keep Ben pinned on the upper level. If he gets a chance to heal in the regeneration chamber on the lower level, this mission gets much more difficult! Keep him at a distance and find a good rhythm between throwing props and using ranged fire attacks. Combined with some lucky explosions of alien objects you should be able to whittle Thing down slowly.

Caution

High mobility is important in this fight. Don't let Thing get close or his super attacks will cause you a lot of hurt!

Cleansing Flame

Objective: Human Torch must destroy all enemies!
Location: NYC Streets
Opponents: Ravagers, Maulers, Desolators

This can be a challenging mission for Human Torch. You face several waves of alien troops with a varied offense. Treat this bonus mission like most other regular missions. You must defeat all enemies that spawn: there are no other objectives.

Pay attention to how the waves progress. When the Maulers show up, you're nearing the end, but don't get careless. Before you kill the last of the Mauler wave, recharge your SP to full. The next wave of Ravagers can be troublesome.

Normal attack combos that juggle into air tackles work very well against Ravagers. Remember that they're trying to lock on to you to fire their energy weapons, so keep moving as much as possible to distract their fire until you take them out one by one.

Tip

Save your SP attacks for eliminating Maulers.

Blazing Speed

Objective: Destroy 20 enemies within 3 minutes, 30 seconds!
Location: The Bridge
Opponents: Ravagers, Decapitators, Maulers

In this last Human Torch bonus mission you definitely have to earn your reward! The name is quite appropriate as well; you must be blazing fast to eliminate all of the opponents within the allotted time limit.

Use mobility attacks (Double-Fisted Air Rams) often. They do a lot of damage (and expend very little SP) especially when combined with impact/fall damage and the odd explosion. This attack is amazing if two or more opponents are lined up, because all of them take impact/fall damage as they're blasted back through the air. Air rams are enough to kill Ravagers should they fly far enough and hit a wall. Super combo attacks work well against Decapitators but they expend too much SP for how many enemies you're facing. Object attacks work great to get you to Rage mode; take advantage of it by using the super mobility attacks (Fireball).

Tip

If you get knocked down, always use your super rising attack to blow away nearby foes.

Human Torch: Sacrifice

Objective: Altered Spider-Man must defeat Human Torch!
Location: Power Plant

This can be one of the hardest sacrifice missions—the Human Torch is no pushover. With all the walls you'd think Spidey would have the upper hand, but Human Torch is just as mobile.

Use your zipline grab to get all the objects you can. Keep them flying at Human Torch to knock him down and always follow-up with Web Bullets—this should do a lot of damage.

Alternately you can take the fight to him with normal and super attack combos. Spidey is a better hand-to-hand fighter than Human Torch, so this tactic works in your favor. Be very wary, though; Human Torch goes into permanent Rage mode at 25 percent health, and from that point he'll do nothing but super mobility attacks.

Throw many objects at Human Torch because he doesn't catch very well. If he does catch it, a timely Web Bullet is a solid backup attack.

Scuttle

Objective: Defeat all enemies and destroy the computer terminal!
Location: Avengers' Mansion
Opponents: Invaders, Decapitators, Obliterators

The first of Iron Man's missions is in two parts. First clear the ground floor of Invaders and Decapitators, and then head down into the lab below the mansion. Once the ground floor waves are eliminated, the force field in the main mansion arena opens up, allowing access to the lab.

Down below is your first Obliterator. These units are tough. They've got heavy armor like Decapitators and energy weapons like Ravagers. You must destroy all the enemies in the lab plus the central computer. Some poles and barrels are lying around in the corners of the lab—use them for object attacks. When the Obliterators are eliminated, there's a final wave of Decapitators just for good measure.

Iron Man's Repulsor Rays are very effective against alien armor—be sure to recharge often so you're never low on SP.

Call of Heroes

Objective: Defend the radar towers!
Location: *Daily Bugle*
Opponents: Invaders, Decapitators, Desolators

You must defend two radar towers in this mission. The first is on the roof of the *Daily Bugle* and the second is on the roof of the darker colored building below. The first tower is attacked by several waves of Invaders and Decapitators. Invaders are very easily eliminated with a normal attack combo that juggles into a normal air tackle. Beat down Decapitators in the same way, but instead use a super air tackle at the end of the combo for more damage. When the first tower is secure, fly down to the lower rooftop and get back to work.

The attacking waves at the second tower consist of Invaders, Decapitators, and Desolators. The same tactics apply here, with the addition of using air tackles for the flying droids. Be persistent, as you have a couple waves to get through, and there's limited room to move on this roof.

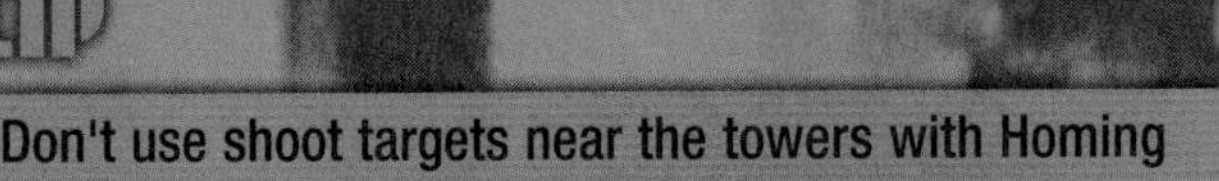

Tip

Don't use shoot targets near the towers with Homing Missiles or Repulsor Rays—the explosions may damage the towers.

The Eternal Soldier

Objective: Iron Man must defeat Brigade!
Location: Power Plant

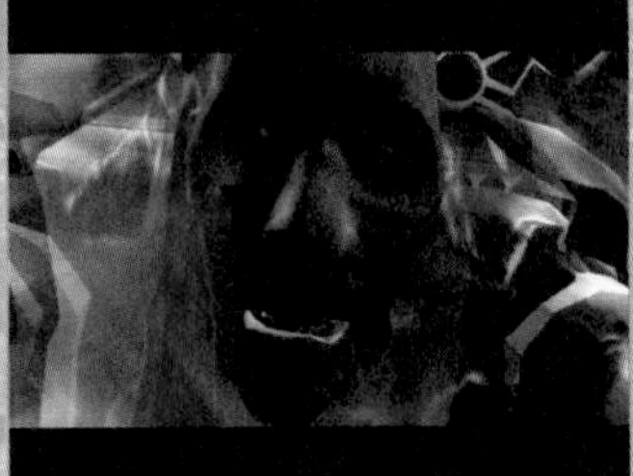

Iron Man literally stumbles across Brigade defending the Power Plant. This mission is an excellent matchup of strong long-range attacks and brute strength combined. Brigade is difficult to beat only if you don't destroy the Tesla Coils that are giving him strength. Throw them at him for some nice initial damage. Until the Tesla Coils are destroyed, Brigade can recharge fully in the power core when it's activated. Super jump attacks and super mobility attacks do a lot of damage against him. When Brigade has drained his SP meter and is having a seizure, hit him hard with explosive objects such as forklifts.

Tip

Brigade draws strength from the Tesla Coils, which allow him to recharge in the power core—destroy them!

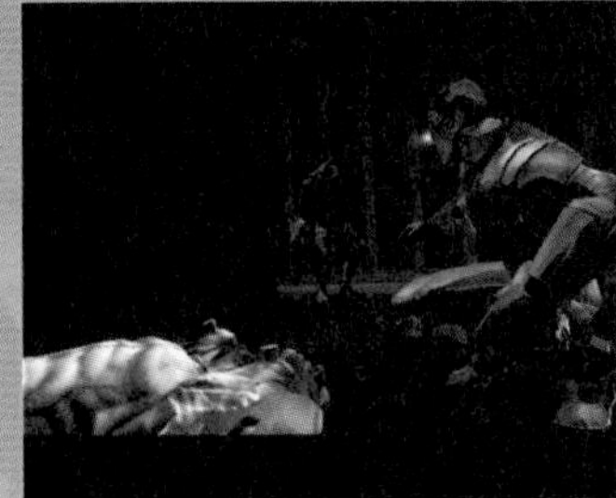

Hot Iron

Objective: Iron Man must defeat Altered Human Torch!
Location: NYC Streets

We found this to be another one of the easiest sacrifice missions. Human Torch primarily uses his ranged attacks, and Iron Man can easily keep him pinned with intermittent Repulsor Blasts that knock Human Torch down. Throw some vehicles into the mix and this should quickly be game over.

Tip

Throw the delivery truck at Human Torch for some incredible damage.

All or Nothing

Objective: Iron Man must defeat all enemies with damaged armor!
Location: Grand Central Station
Opponents: Invaders, Ravagers, Desolators

This is, hands down, the game's toughest bonus mission. Iron Man's armor is damaged and you start with almost zero health. You must face and destroy a wave of Invaders, Ravagers, and Desolators! The amount of damage Iron Man can withstand in this mission is limited: one hit from an object, one hit from a flying Desolator, or two physical attacks from either of the ground units.

Tons of objects are lying around, and the upper level of the arena is open as well. You need all this room to move and to hide when you're recharging. Use your SP efficiently in this level—don't waste energy on extraneous movements. Fly to where you want to go and then hang out on the ground to recharge. Patience pays off royally here; don't rush into any confrontation if the balance isn't in your favor. It's better to retreat and come back strong than to get blown away completely.

Tip

Use all of the objects to launch attacks against the alien troops. This tactic helps save precious SP and keeps opponents at long range where they can't damage you further.

Iron Man: Sacrifice

Objective: Van Roekel must defeat Iron Man!
Location: Avengers' Mansion

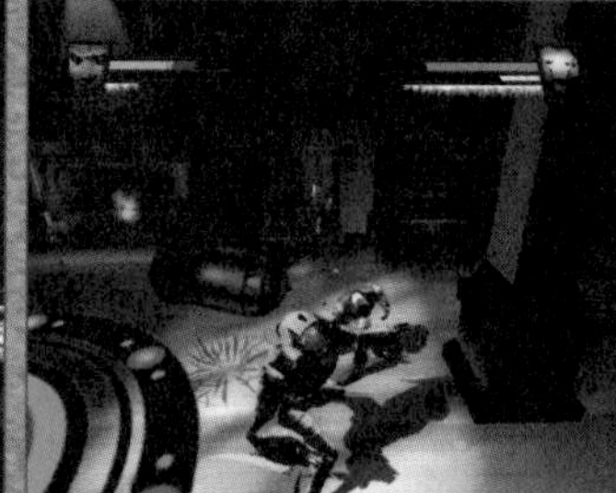

Van Roekel confronts Iron Man right in his own backyard! Here in the Avengers' Mansion you can bet things are going to get heated fast! The Minuteman armor may just be the greatest threat Iron Man has ever seen in an opponent.

Van Roekel's super ranged attack is far superior to Iron Man's, so blast him often, but pay close attention to your SP meter. Van Roekel is more than a match for Iron Man. If you play smart there's no way you can lose.

Tip

Air combos and rising attacks are less effective because Iron Man has such high defenses.

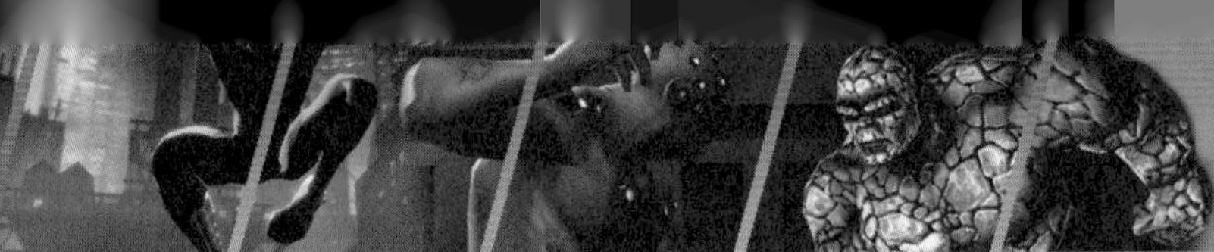

MAGNETO

MASTER OF MAGNETISM

Location: Power Plant
Opponents: Invaders, Obliterators, Predators

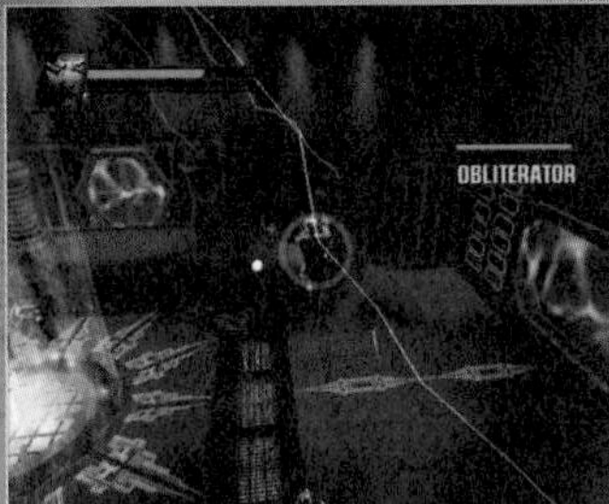

Magneto's first objective in the Power Plant arena is to destroy (or take offline) the many Tesla Coils powering the force field over the exit door. There is a dangerous mix of alien troops here with powerful ranged attacks, so don't stay in the open for too long. Drop down and hide behind a Tesla Coil, throw it, then hover over the next one and repeat until they're all offline or destroyed.

When the cutscene ends, use your magnetic pull on the door to destroy it and reveal a passage. Eliminate the several Ravagers ahead in the passage and two more in the far room. Crush the far door and proceed through to complete the mission.

TIP

You don't have to destroy the Tesla Coils. Just topple them so they're not contributing to the force field protecting the exit passage.

DEATH INCARNATE

Location: NYC Streets
Opponents: Desolators, Maulers, Obliterators

You start off in the old back alley, and right away two Desolators attack from through the fire. Hover and air tackle them for easy kills. The few more Desolators and a wave of Maulers out in the open street section are fairly simple to eliminate with super throws and object attacks. Quickly throw all the props you can by using the magnetic pull ability.

Destroy the wave of aliens in the open street section before the force field on the far passage deactivates. When the force field drops, another wave of aliens, including Obliterators, spawns and attacks. If you haven't used the tank yet, now is a good time. Eliminate this wave and proceed into the alley to end the mission.

TIP

Be cautious picking up the tank to hurl at your opponents. If an obstacle is in the way, it can either break the tank into pieces or explode it before you can toss it away.

POISONED STEEL

Objective: Magneto must defeat Hazmat!
Location: Grand Central Station

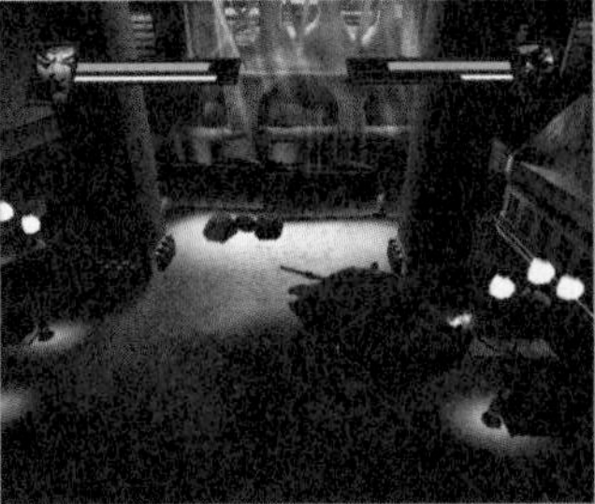

Hazmat dares challenge the Master of Magnetism? Who does this toxic waste dump think he is? To worsen the insult, Hazmat poisoned Magneto with toxic spew just prior to the fight, so keep in mind that you're constantly losing health!

Don't feel inclined to fight him fairly. Crush him into a green chunky stew with large heavy objects: chunks of concrete and the tank, for example. If he's on the ground, super throws work very well too. Either way, just don't get confused by his high mobility. Be conservative and let him come to you.

TIP

Hazmat doesn't catch very well—hurl many objects at him to beat him down! If you hit him with the tank twice, he'll be down for the count or very nearly finished off.

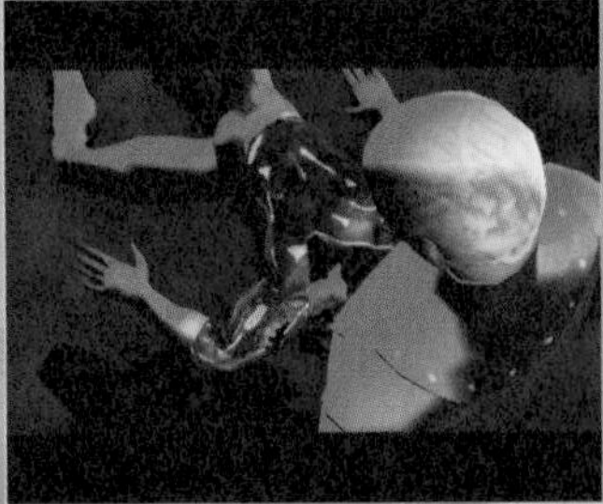

Magneto: Sacrifice

Objective: Paragon must defeat Magneto!
Location: Grand Central Station

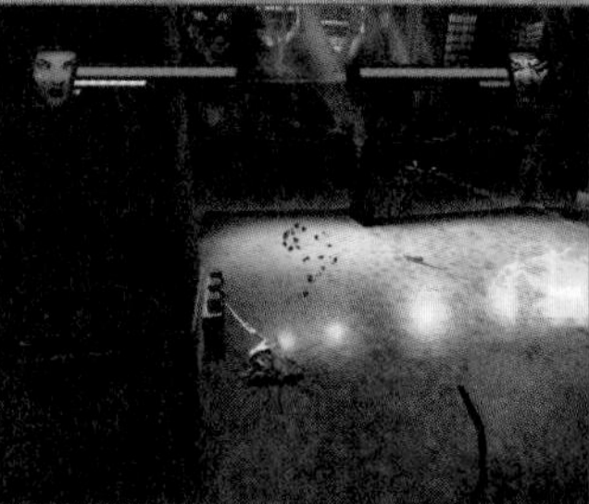

The Duel of Masters is an appropriate name for this battle. Paragon is the pinnacle of Van Roekel's research and development into the perfect warrior. And Magneto is one of the most powerful mutants alive.

Magneto usually hovers as long as he can—this makes for easy super air tackles. Use your long-range attacks, and be sure to get in close for some normal and super attack combos. Paragon makes mincemeat out of Magneto in hand-to-hand combat.

Tip

One direct hit with the tank is nearly all you need to defeat Magneto.

Paragon

Beta Test

Objective: Destroy all Turlin Engines within the time limits for each stage!
Location: Van Roekel's Headquarters

Paragon's first chance to stretch her legs is a very straightforward exercise in destruction. The many Turlin Engines along this corridor in Van Roekel's Headquarters must be destroyed within the time limit.

Turlin Engines are easily destroyed by regular attack combos, ascending jump attacks, and even ranged attacks. When you see a group of engines, try using the super ranged attack to damage a few in one shot. Watch for the alien "lampposts"; use these as hurling weapons to quickly destroy their targets. You may have to super jump across one of the gaps when moving across the blue energy platforms.

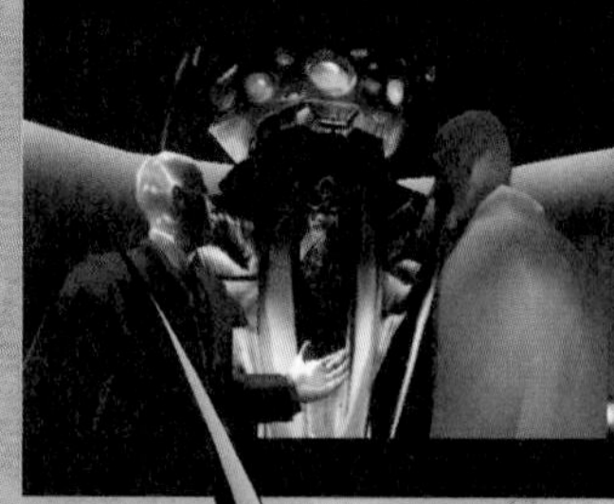

Maya's Dilemma

Location: Van Roekel's Headquarters
Opponents: Eviscerators, Ravagers

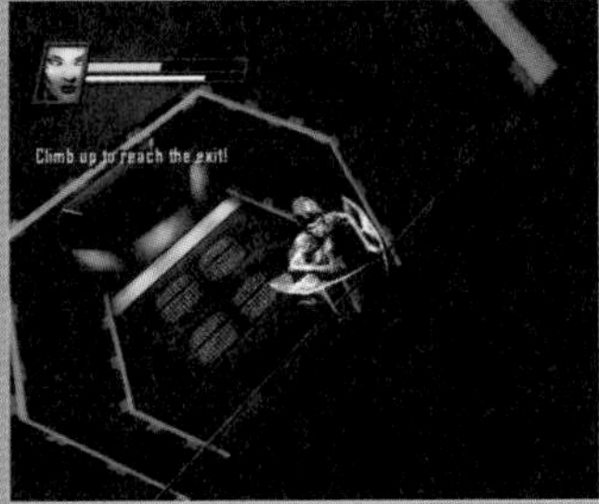

Maya has escaped—now she needs to book it out of Van Roekel's Headquarters! A horde of Eviscerators and Ravagers awaits between you and the exit, but luckily it can be done in small stages. Several times you're isolated by a force field, doorway, or energy wall and confronted by another wave of aliens.

Normal attack combos work well against Eviscerators. Save your SP for long-range energy attacks against Ravagers, which kills them almost outright when they are blasted back into the walls. As you proceed down the corridor, you see some blue doors in several energy walls—they must be destroyed. Jump throw the objects lying around at the higher doors. When you finally reach the end of the hallway, wall climb out a vertical passage leading up to complete the mission.

Paragon's Revenge

Location: Van Roekel's Headquarters
Opponents: Decapitators, Obliterators, Maulers

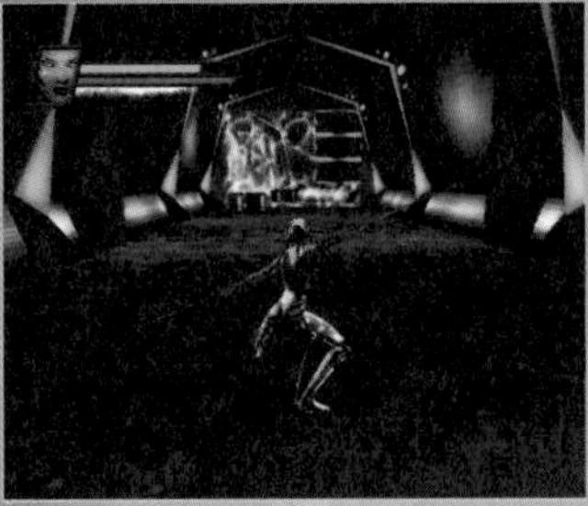

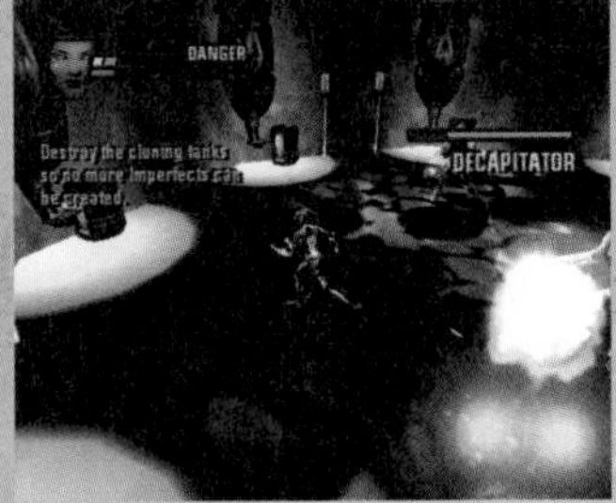

Paragon is on a crusade to destroy the cloning tanks so that no more Imperfects can be created. Unfortunately there is a small army of the most hardcore alien troops between you and the cloning facilities. This difficult mission requires some tact—most specifically, save your SP for ranged attacks against groups of aliens and to teleport out of sticky situations!

Use mobility attacks (Teleport) often to keep the Obliterators from getting a bead on you with their energy weapons. Always eliminate them first when fighting a group of aliens. Use all the objects you can find and keep throwing them to cause explosions. Destroy the cloning facility and the tanks at end of the hall to complete the mission.

Meet Your Maker

Objective: Paragon must defeat Van Roekel!
Location: Van Roekel's Headquarters

This is the final showdown between Paragon and her creator, Niles Van Roekel. The Minuteman armor Van Roekel created has significant components of the same abilities he put into his perfect warrior: high mobility, durability, and firepower. Thankfully Paragon has one up on him in that her melee attacks are more effective. Normal attack combos are fast and don't use up your valuable SP meter.

To beat Van Roekel easily, keep him pinned on the upper level or he will continue to chain heal himself in the regeneration chamber. To keep him pinned, throw or swat many objects at him and hope for chain reaction explosions to increase the damage. When he finally lands, follow up with super ranged attacks, which also knock him around. Watch for the large alien land mines to respawn and keep throwing them at him; direct hits do impressive damage. If you run out of things to throw, get in close and outfight him in hand-to-hand combat using dodge attacks—he won't stick around too long for that but you may get some good hits in. The key to beating Van Roekel is just to keep the pressure on—don't ever let up.

Tip: Keeping hitting Van Roekel with the large alien land mines to keep his health down.

arenas

the bridge

SPECIAL HAZARD
Ring Out

SPECIAL HAZARD
Falling Rubble

Walkway

Retaining Wall

SPECIAL HAZARD
Falling Rubble

SPECIAL HAZARD
Flame Jets

SPECIAL HAZARD
Ring Out

Setting

The Brooklyn Bridge has been nearly destroyed by the alien invaders—heavy fire from their ships has reduced most of it to rubble. Here is one last standing section, partially destroyed and teetering above the river.

The Bridge is a well-balanced arena for all fighter styles. It offers retaining walls for wall-runners, upper walls in the back of the arena for wall-climbers, open air for fliers, and tons of debris for heroes who prefer to stay on the ground and hurl barrels and cars at their foes.

Weapons and Objects

Class 1: Barrels, pipes (on platform walls)
Class 2: Metal crates, cars, taxis, lampposts
Class 3: Semi

Special Hazards

1. Flame Jets: Watch for the three locations along the cracks in the bridge surface that spew forth massive jets of flame. Each location fires intermittently and will combust or explode anything on top of it—which could be you or various objects.
2. Ring Out: Over the sides of both retaining walls there's nothing but open air down to the river. When you're near the wall try super throwing your opponent over it to score a ring-out victory.
3. Falling Rubble: Every so often chucks of the bridge fall off and crush anything underneath them. If the rubble hits something combustible it sets off an explosion—don't get caught in a chain reaction!

Strategy

Weaker characters can use the raised ramp at the arena's center/back to confuse stronger opponents. Keep it between you and your foes while regaining stamina and composure. The elevation difference lets you launch high jumping attacks down on your opponents' heads. Or wait for them to climb up to your level and then blast them off the platform with super attacks or weapons.

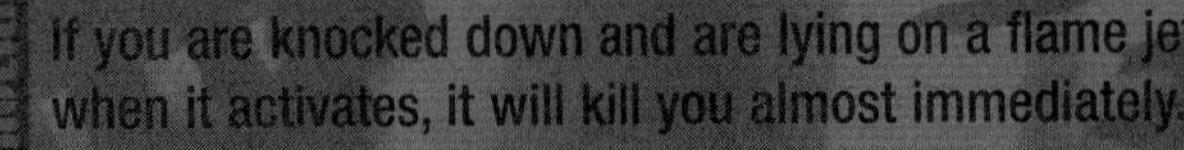

Caution

If you are knocked down and are lying on a flame jet when it activates, it will kill you almost immediately.

Ring-Out Procedure

1

2

3

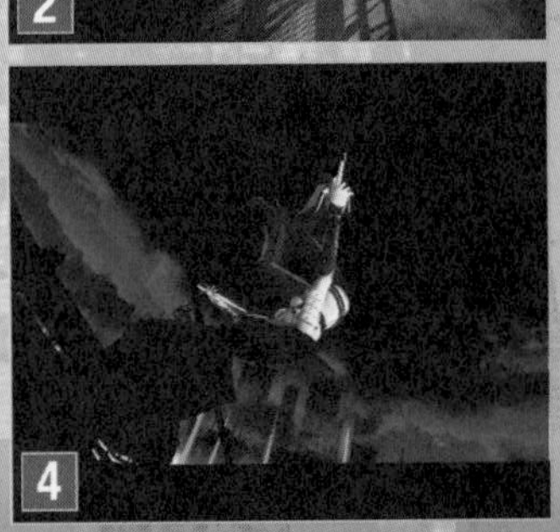

4

5

Arenas

NYC Streets

Setting

The streets of New York City are likely the most common venue for superhero brawls—as any comic book fan could tell you. Here the dreams come true! This square arena is closed in by the high walls of the surrounding buildings. Some of the storefronts are destructible, and weapons and objects litter the street.

This arena is another fair proving ground for any style of hero: wall space for climbers and runners, open air for fliers, and never a shortage of weapons and projectiles for the ground fighters who just want to rip something out of the ground to throw at their opponents.

Caution

Some of the surrounding walls are not climbable due to their irregular surfaces and angles.

Weapons and Objects

Class 1: Parking meters, newspaper boxes, barrels, pipes
Class 2: Garbage bins, lampposts, taxis
Class 3: Delivery truck

Note

There are no special hazards in the NYC Streets arena.

Strategy

This arena is very open, so use your mobility moves often. At ground level there isn't much between you and your opponent, so use the arena's height to your advantage: Super jump, wall crawl, wall run, and fly to get the drop on your enemies.

All the debris in the streets makes this a dangerous arena when fighting a powerful ground fighter such as The Thing. Many of the objects are explosive or can explode the surrounding objects on impact. Rely heavily on mobility moves to dodge quickly!

arenas

Avengers' Mansion

SPECIAL HAZARD
Gas Lamps

SPECIAL HAZARD
Painting

SPECIAL HAZARD
Painting

SPECIAL HAZARD
Columns

SPECIAL HAZARD
Columns

Setting

This long-standing bastion of heroism in NYC has been attacked and partially destroyed by the alien invaders. The great inner room is still standing at least, and this is where you face off against your opponents. The arena is full of large concrete columns you can throw your foes through, and the walls are lined with bookshelves that blast apart on impact.

With such a high degree of destructibility, this level provides more serious threats from flying debris, explosions, weapons, and thrown objects than the previous two arenas. Wall-runners, climbers, and fliers have an advantage here due to their higher mobility combined with the length of the arena. Slower ground fighters will become weary from going back and forth from end to end repeatedly.

Weapons and Objects

Class 1: Tables, chairs, sofas, pikes (from suits of armor), armor, display cases
Class 2: Bookcases, gas lamps
Class 3: Concrete columns (once broken)

Special Hazards

1. Gas Lamps: These explosive fixtures start the fight attached to their ceiling mounts. During the battle, the fall to the floor and come to rest where they may. If a gas lamp should fall on one already below, it may cause an explosion. These make for excellent throwing weapons due to their volatile nature.
2. Paintings: When disturbed, these paintings fall off the walls causing damage. Throw your opponents into the walls below them for this added effect.
3. Columns: Toss your foes through these columns for damage and when the concrete sections are on the floor, pick them up and use them as weapons.

Strategy

This arena starts off more enclosed and difficult to maneuver in due to all of the columns, railings, and furniture. However, once it's cleared of objects, it feels more like a warehouse with plenty of room to move.

The concrete columns are the only Class 3 weapon in the arena. If you're fighting a hero who is strong enough to pick up one of these columns after it's toppled, get out of there quickly! Thrown or wielded columns cause critical damage.

If you're playing a hero with high mobility, use the full length of this arena to your advantage. Keep moving to the far end and make your opponent come to you—this gives you ample time to set up your attacks or even to recover from damage before the next clash.

ARENAS

Daily Bugle

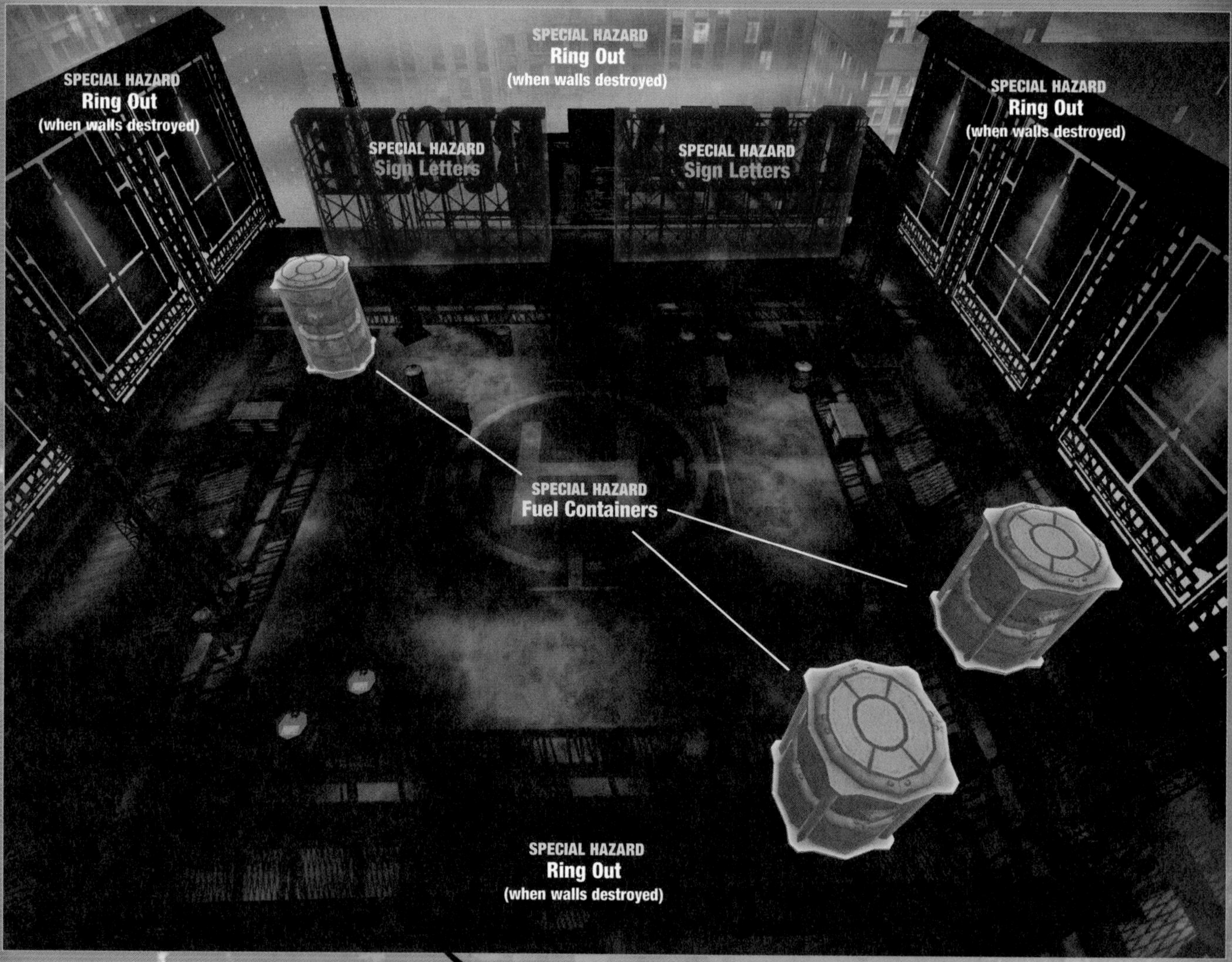

SPECIAL HAZARD
Ring Out
(when walls destroyed)

SPECIAL HAZARD
Ring Out
(when walls destroyed)

SPECIAL HAZARD
Ring Out
(when walls destroyed)

SPECIAL HAZARD
Sign Letters

SPECIAL HAZARD
Sign Letters

SPECIAL HAZARD
Fuel Containers

SPECIAL HAZARD
Ring Out
(when walls destroyed)

Setting

The rooftop of the *Daily Bugle* building is a good place to brawl high above the city—and it's a long way down! This arena is initially walled in by the *Daily Bugle* sign on one side and framed metal walls on the other three, but all four sides are destructible! Fliers will be at home here, as will ground fighters with all of the objects littering the rooftop.

Weapons and Objects

Class 1: Barrels, pipes, air conditioners
Class 2: Sign letters, metal bins
Class 3: Radio towers, fuel containers

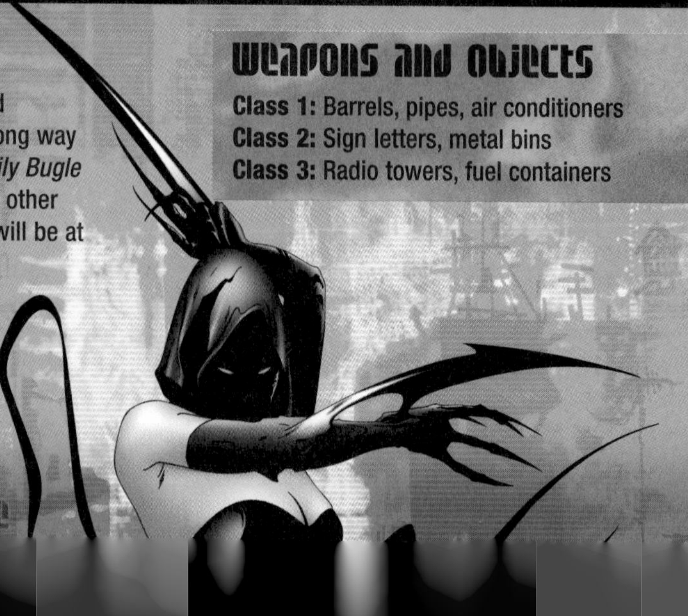

Strategy

Destroy the walls as soon as possible to increase the ring-out hazard. Just make sure this isn't used against you. Super throws near the open areas created by destroyed walls can cause a ring out. Toss your opponent off the building for a victory!

Explosions on this level can be fatal if they blow you out of the arena. If you're playing against a strong fighter who can hurl the large fuel containers, stay near the middle once the walls are destroyed to avoid a blast that could hurl you out of the arena. That being said, don't spend too much time near the edge regardless of who you're fighting—one lucky juggling technique or power punch and you're off on a one-way ride to street level.

Wall-runners and wall-climbers initially have a great advantage in this arena—take full advantage of it before the walls are destroyed and your advantage is gone. Stronger players find no shortage of objects for throwing or wielding. The fuel canisters and radio towers are devastating weapons, but use them wisely as they don't respawn. Fuel canisters make for easy ring outs if the walls have been destroyed and the explosion catches your opponent off guard. Try to save these for when the walls are gone, as the explosions often cause ring outs.

Special Hazards

1. Ring Out: Once the sign and walls are destroyed, there is a very high risk of ring outs on the rooftop. Depending on your character and play style, this can be good or very, very bad news.
2. *Daily Bugle* Sign: When the sign takes enough damage, letters fall off to the rooftop, which are then available as weapons. Keep in mind that they can do you damage if they fall off the sign onto you, if you're thrown into them.
3. Fuel Containers: These Class 3 weapons can only be picked up by the strongest characters; however, they can still be damaged enough to explode. When you see them flaming, move away: A huge explosion is about to happen!

Ring-Out Procedure

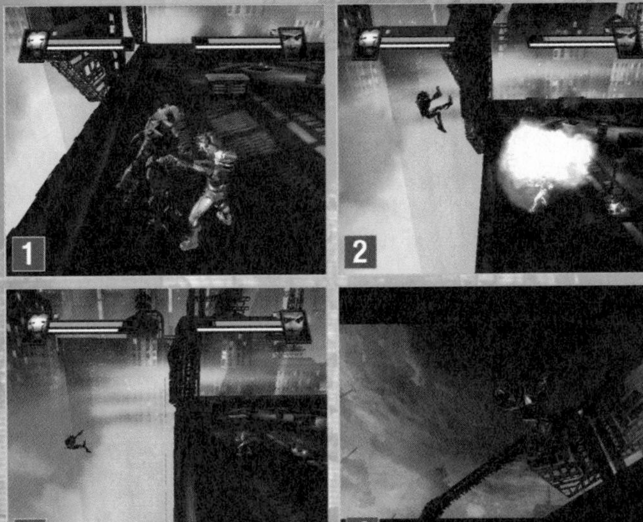
1 2 3 4

5

arenas

Grand Central Station

SPECIAL HAZARD
Ring Out
(after barriers destroyed)

SPECIAL HAZARD
Columns

Setting

Grand Central Station is an underground arena, showing obvious signs of the alien attack. Parts of the roof have been destroyed, and the lower levels are exposed by recent explosions. This arena is quite open, giving quick characters some advantage over stronger and more powerful foes.

Wall-runners and crawlers have a definite advantage here with so much indestructible wall space. There are also plenty of objects for wielding as weapons or throwing—including a full-size tank that only a few incredibly strong characters can use.

Weapons and Objects

Class 1: Barrels, newspaper boxes, benches, railings
Class 2: Telephones, lockers, lampposts
Class 3: Tank, concrete column debris

Strategy

More powerful heroes should destroy the large concrete columns to gain a full line of sight. A clear shot is incredibly valuable when hurling objects at opponents. Take away their hiding places first, then blast 'em with some big concrete blocks!

Wall-runners should use the indestructible walls to their fullest advantage. Launch relentless walls attacks to keep your opponent off balance. Mix it up with close-in super attacks, then return to the walls to regroup.

Special Hazards

1. Ring Out: Check out the abyss at the rear of the level. The concrete barriers here can be destroyed, opening up a significant hazard on this end of the arena.
2. Concrete Columns: These large columns can be broken down into several large chunks of concrete that only the strongest characters are able to lift. When the column breaks, dive out of the way so the collapsing blocks don't crush you.

Ring-Out Procedure

1

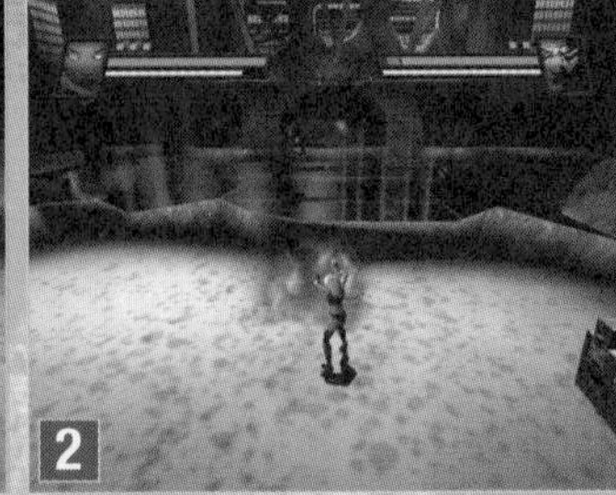

2

3

4

5

ARENAS

POWER PLANT

Setting

This fully contained arena is set within a two-level power plant chamber filled with tons of hazardous materials, industrial equipment, and explosives. Many objects here help ground fighters clobber weaker fighters and stop the high-mobility characters in their tracks.

The walls are indestructible, so runners and crawlers have a permanent advantage here; however, anyone with high mobility can safely get from one side to the other very quickly. The upper level makes for an excellent height advantage to fight from.

Weapons and Objects

Class 1: Barrels, pipes
Class 2: Computer terminals, forklifts, propane canisters, metal crates
Class 3: Tesla coils, column pieces

Tip The power core can be used to recharge your health to full if the timing is perfect. Just before it turns on, if you are in the air over it, you will be zapped to full health. Your health is restored to full, but your Stamina meter will be low. Again, timing is critical, especially for characters who can't fly and have to time their jumps.

Special Hazards

1. Power Core: This electrical circuit intermittently hums on and off throughout your battles. Anyone caught inside when it turns on receives critical damage. Alternately, if you hit the outside of the core after it's activated you receive less damage.
2. Steel Columns: Like those of Grand Central Station, they can be broken—causing damage to anyone hit by the debris. Only the strongest characters will be able to use the debris as weapons.

Strategy

The power core in the arena's center causes extremely high damage to unsuspecting heroes—plan for this! It should be a part of every fighter's strategy inside the Power Plant—well-timed attacks send your opponent inside the core when it activates! Even bumping up against it from the outside will cause damage while it's pulsating with intense current.

Use super jump or mobility moves to access the higher level above the main floor. From there you can launch attacks with a height advantage that adds damage to your attacks (fall damage). Lure your opponent up there and attack relentlessly before he gets a foothold on the edge. Also, it's a clear shot to the lower level with projectiles or hurled weapons.

Powerful fighters do well in this arena with so many objects (many of them are Class 2 and 3) to hurl at reckless foes. Keep moving and throw everything you can get your hands on.

Arenas

Van Roekel's Headquarters

SPECIAL HAZARD
Force Walls

SPECIAL HAZARD
Alien Landmines

SPECIAL FEATURE
Regeneration Chamber

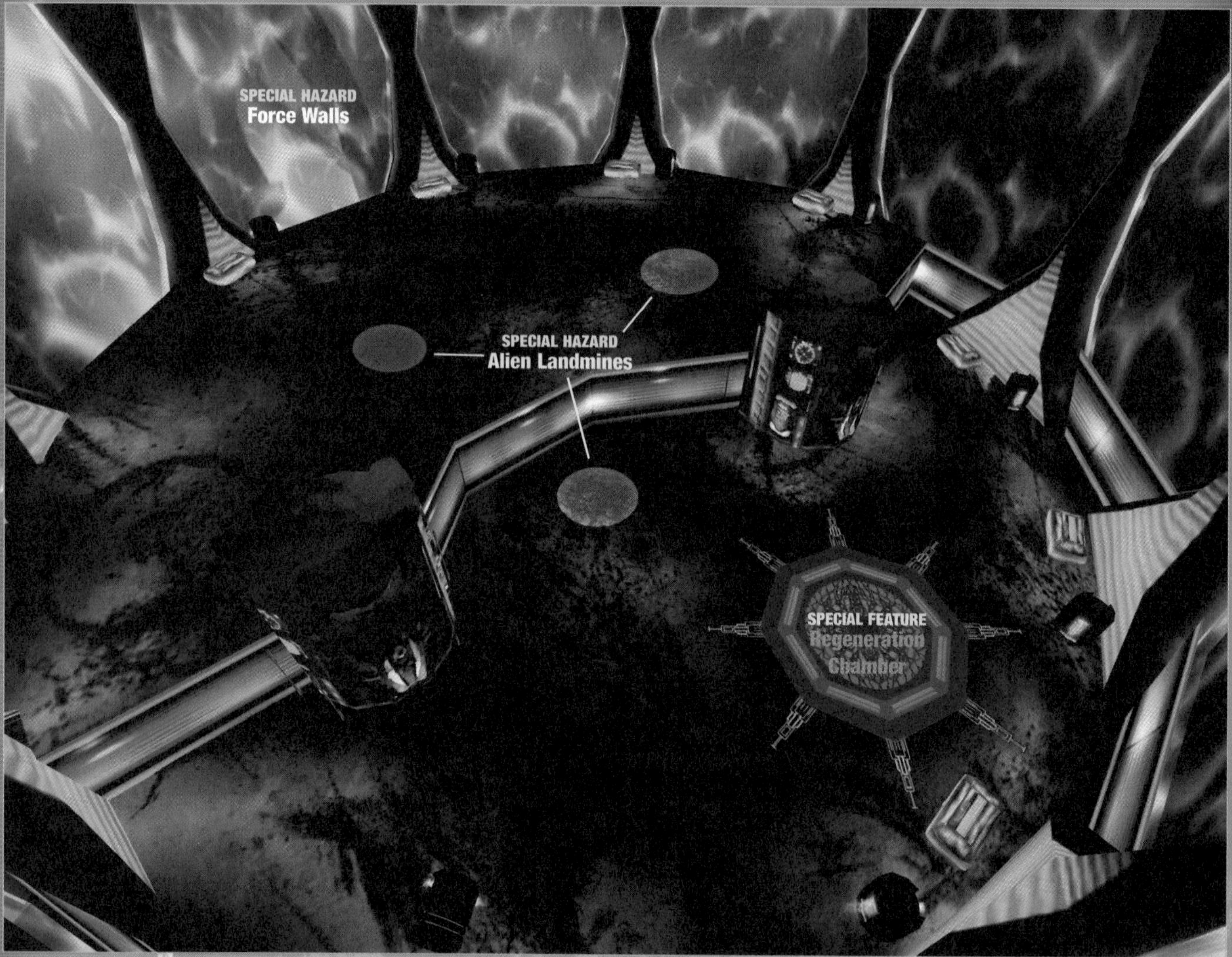

Setting

This is the ultimate alien warrior testing grounds. Van Roekel's Headquarters houses the latest alien technology in his training facility. The place has a futuristic feel and comes with many built-in hazards and features.

The high spherical environment gives nearly equal opportunities for all types of character, with the exception of wall-runners who are inhibited by the force walls surrounding the arena.

Weapons and Objects

Class 1: Alien containers, fuel cells, pipes (taken from sides of large weapons dispensers on ground floor)
Class 2: None
Class 3: Alien landmines

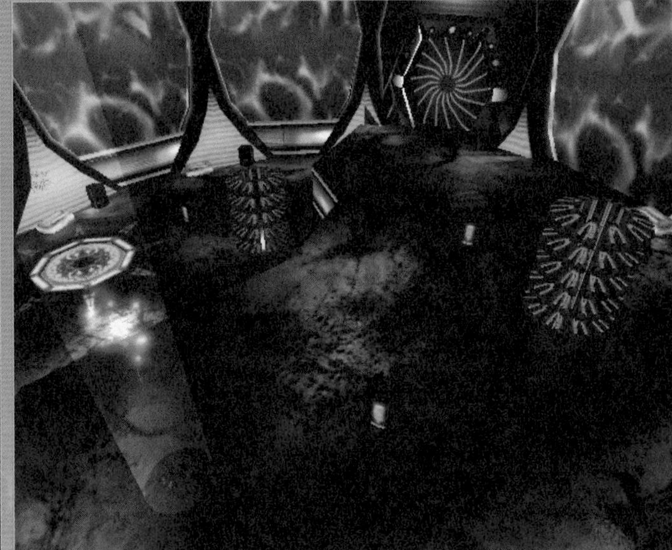

SPECIAL HAZARDS

1. Alien Landmines: These stacked land mines smolder inside the cylinder for brief periods before their massive explosions. If you time it right, one can be picked up and hurled like a giant grenade. In this case, it explodes upon impact.
2. Force Walls: The arena's force walls are highly charged, and they damage all who touch them.
3. Red Teleporters (not shown on map): The only thing that comes down these red beams are fireballs! When you see a beam appear, get out of the way!

SPECIAL FEATURES

1. White Teleporters (not shown on map): These consistently beam in new objects to use as weapons. There is rarely a shortage of items to hurl at your opponents.
2. Regeneration Chamber: When this device is activated, step inside the lit area to recharge your health. The chamber activates intermittently, so be ready to use it during the short time it's on. Use any tactic you can to keep your opponent out of it!

STRATEGY

Avoid chain reaction explosions! Even if you're not the strongest character, clear the area of all objects you can throw. Chain reactions cause a pinball effect with devastating results.

Wall-runners must rely on the other aspects of their high mobility. Any attempt to access the walls results in a painful shock from the force walls.

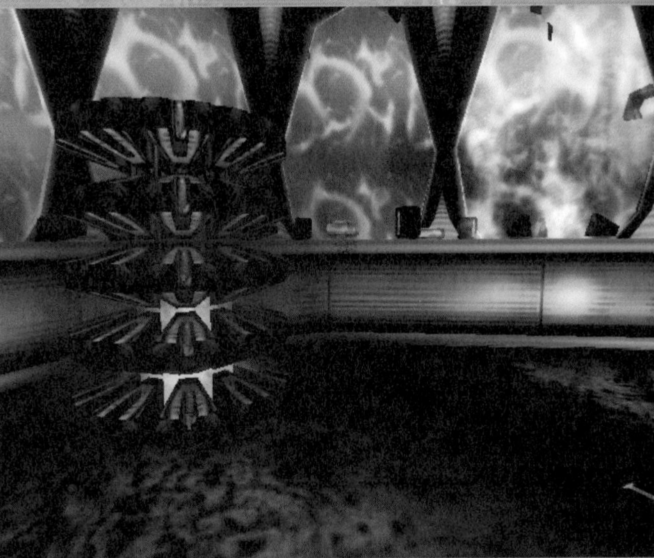

ONLINE PLAY

EA game fans will immediately recognize the online system as the one used across all EA titles. The setup and orientation are much the same, with options for Quick Match, OptiMatch, Lobby, Stats, and My Marvel.

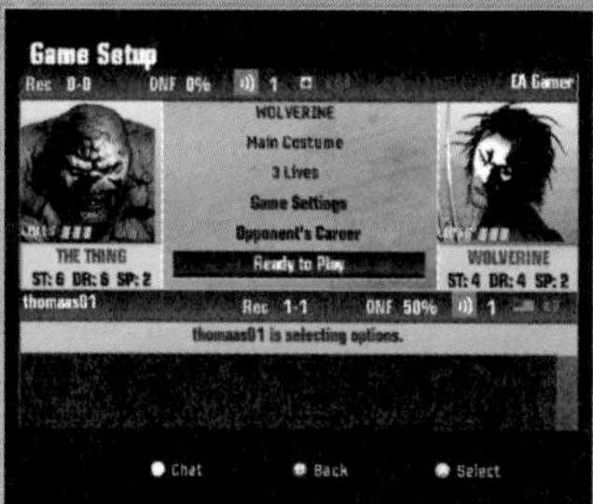

Quick Matches and OptiMatches are where you'll set up your games. You can choose game type, venue, Maximum DNF % (Did Not Finish), and skill level of your potential opponents. On the game setup screen, you choose your specific options: character, lives, and alternate costumes (the altered versions of the characters). Use the Opponent's Career option to view your opponent's record and learn about his or her strategy.

In the Lobby, you find various rooms that may be categorized by skill level and DNF %.

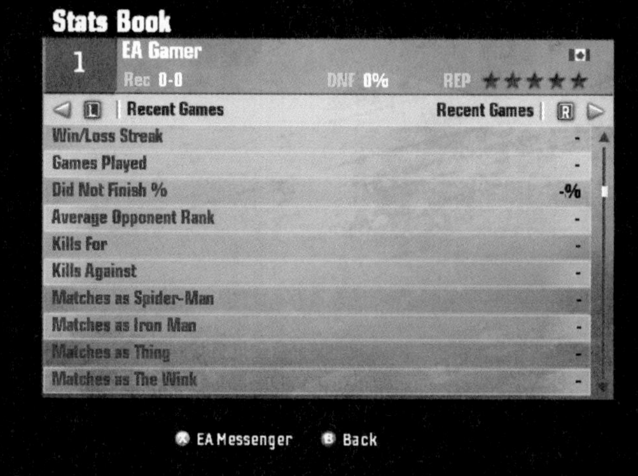

Use the Stats Book to review your win/loss record and DNF %. Other stats include total games played, average opponent ranks, kills for, kills against, and matches played as individual characters. Everything you need to know about your career is listed here.

The Top 100 list is the comprehensive leader board for *Marvel Nemesis*. It tracks the players ranked in the top 100, by ranking points that are earned and lost in a similar system as chess ranking. New players are given a bank of points, and you can win points to increase your rank by beating other players or you can lose points by being beaten.

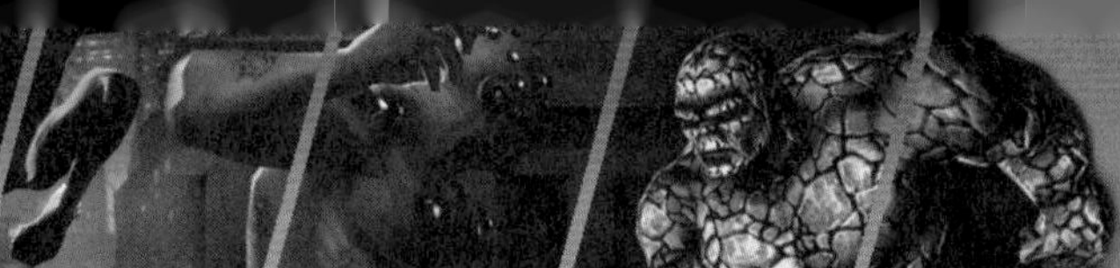

Cheats and Rewards

Cheats

Enter these cheats in the options/cheats menus:

Cheat Code	Code Effect
SAVAGELAND	Unlock all Fantastic Four comics
NZONE	Unlock all Tomorrow People comics
THEHAND	Unlock Electra swimsuit card
REIKO	Unlock Solara swimsuit card
MONROE	Unlock Storm swimsuit card

Note: Every 10 matches in Versus mode unlock either a character or an arena; however, no cards or comics are unlocked in Versus mode.

Story Mode Rewards

The rewards that are unlocked in Story mode consist of arenas, cards, characters, comics, and movies. They are listed generally by character progression in Story mode. The order in which you unlock the following items is largely determined by the order you play the Story mode missions.

Rewards Table

Mission	Unlock Reward
Thing 1	Card—Niles Van Roekel
Thing 2	Card—Invaders
Thing 3	Card—Thing
Thing 4 Bonus	Comic 1—Fantastic Four
Thing 5 Bonus	Comic 2—Fantastic Four
Thing Sacrifice	Card—Thing's Final Stand; Movie—Fault Zone Background
Wolverine 1	Card—Wolverine
Wolverine 2	Card—Avengers' Mansion
Wolverine 3	Card—Wink
Wolverine 4 Bonus	Comic 3—Fantastic Four
Wolverine 5 Bonus	Comic 4—Fantastic Four
Wolverine Sacrifice	Card—Beasts of War; Movie—Brigade Background
Elektra 1	Card—Elektra
Elektra 2	Card—*Daily Bugle*
Elektra 3	Card—Eviscerators
Elektra 4 Bonus	Comic 5—Fantastic Four
Elektra 5 Bonus	Comic 6—Fantastic Four
Elektra Sacrifice	Card—Femmes Fatales; Movie—Wink Background
Daredevil 1	Card—Daredevil
Daredevil 2	Arena—Grand Central Station
Daredevil 3	Card—Johnny Ohm; Character—Daredevil (Versus mode)
Daredevil 4 Bonus	Comic 7—Fantastic Four
Daredevil 5 Bonus	Comic 8—Fantastic Four
Daredevil Sacrifice	Card—Devil's Fire; Movie—Solara Background
Storm 1	Card—Storm
Storm 2	Card—Desolators
Storm 3	Card—Fault Zone; Character—Storm (Versus mode); Character—Fault Zone (Versus mode)
Storm 4 Bonus	Comic 9—Fantastic Four
Storm 5 Bonus	Comic 1—Tomorrow People
Storm Sacrifice	Card—Van Roekel's Laboratory
Venom 1	Card—Venom
Venom 2	Card—Turlin Neural Override
Venom 3	Card—Solara; Character—Venom (Versus mode); Character—Solara (Versus mode)
Venom 4 Bonus	Comic 2—Tomorrow People
Venom 5 Bonus	Comic 3—Tomorrow People
Venom Sacrifice	Card—Lethal Toxin; Movie—Hazmat Background
Spider-Man 1	Card—Spider-Man
Spider-Man 2	Card—Maulers
Spider-Man 3	Arena—*Daily Bugle*
Spider-Man 4 Bonus	Comic 4—Tomorrow People
Spider-Man 5 Bonus	Comic 5—Tomorrow People
Spider-Man Sacrifice	Card—High Voltage; Movie—Johnny Ohm Background
Human Torch 1	Card—Human Torch
Human Torch 2	Card—Turlin Engine
Human Torch 3	Arena—Van Roekel's Headquarters
Human Torch 4 Bonus	Comic 6—Tomorrow People
Human Torch 5 Bonus	Comic 7—Tomorrow People
Human Torch Sacrifice	Card—Obliterators
Iron Man 1	Card—Iron Man
Iron Man 2	Card—Van Roekel Battle Suit
Iron Man 3	Card—Brigade; Arena—Power Plant; Character—Brigade (Versus mode); Character—Iron Man (Versus mode)
Iron Man 4 Bonus	Comic 8—Tomorrow People
Iron Man 5 Bonus	Comic 9—Tomorrow People
Iron Man Sacrifice	Card—Iron and Steel
Magneto 1	Card—Magneto
Magneto 2	Card—Paragon
Magneto 3	Card—Hazmat; Character—Hazmat (Versus mode); Character—Magneto (Versus mode)
Magneto Sacrifice	Card—Clash of Masters
Paragon 1	Card—Maya
Paragon 2	Card—Flight to Freedom; Movie—Paragon Background
Paragon 3	Character—Paragon (Versus mode)
Paragon 4	Card—Paragon Meets Her Maker; Character—Van Roekel (Versus mode)

It's 2:00AM and you're about to be killed for the 11th time tonight

TURN TO PRIMA EGUIDES
WE ARE NEVER CLOSED

• HIDDEN GUNS & AMMO • COMPLETE BOSS BATTLE SOLUTIONS • FULL MAPS
• DETAILED STRATEGY • OVER 350 EGUIDES FOR YOUR FAVORITE GAMES
www.primagames.com